THE BIG BOOK OF SEARCH AND FIND

By
Tony Tallarico

kidsbooks
Incorporated

FIND FREDDIE

WHERE ARE THEY?

Find Freddie along with hundreds of other zany things in these hilarious scenes.

- Uncle Sam at the ballpark
- Cowboys on the beach
- Humpty Dumpty in Monsterville
- Balloons at the movies
- Flying fish in space
- Peanuts at the museum
- Rabbits at school
- Flying saucers in the Old West

. . . and lots more!

FIND FREDDIE
AT HOME AND ...

- Alligator
- Apple
- Big foot
- Bird's nest
- Boxing glove
- Bug
- Cupcake
- Deflated balloon
- Dinosaur
- 4 Drumsticks
- Eight ball
- Electric guitar
- False teeth
- Fire hydrant
- Football helmet
- Footprints
- Giant pencil
- "Goof Off" medal
- 2 Hamburgers
- Lifesaver
- 2 Locomotives
- Magnifying glass
- Mailbox
- Model plane
- Monster hand
- Mouse house
- 3 Music notes
- Paintbrush
- Ping-pong net
- "Quarantine"
- Sled
- Slice of pizza
- Snake
- Soccer ball
- 3 Speakers
- Tent
- Thermometer
- "Think Small"
- 13:15
- Top hat
- Toy car
- Tricycle
- "Yech!"
- Yo-yo

FIND FREDDIE
IN SPACE AND . . .

- ☒ Alien basketball player
- ☒ Barbell
- ☒ Barber
- ☒ 2 Bats
- ☒ Bow tie
- ☒ Butterfly
- ☒ Cow
- ☒ Crayon
- ☒ Dragon
- ☒ Dunce cap
- ☒ Earmuffs
- ☐ Elephant
- ☒ 2 Feet
- ☒ Firecracker
- ☒ 2 Flying fish
- ☒ Flying horse
- ☒ Hammer
- ☒ Happy face
- ☒ 4 Hot dogs
- ☒ Igloo
- ☒ Kite
- ☒ 10 Moons
- ☒ Moviemaker
- ☒ Nose
- ☒ Owl
- ☒ P.D.
- ☒ Part of a star
- ☒ Peter Pan
- ☒ Pinocchio
- ☒ Pig
- ☒ Pizza
- ☒ Planet Earth
- ☒ Santa Claus
- ☒ Seal
- ☒ Skateboard
- ☒ Skull planet
- ☒ Space cat
- ☒ "Stairwars"
- ☒ Submarine
- ☒ Sunglasses
- ☒ Telescope
- ☒ Traffic signal
- ☒ Truck
- ☒ Tulips
- ☒ Two-headed alien

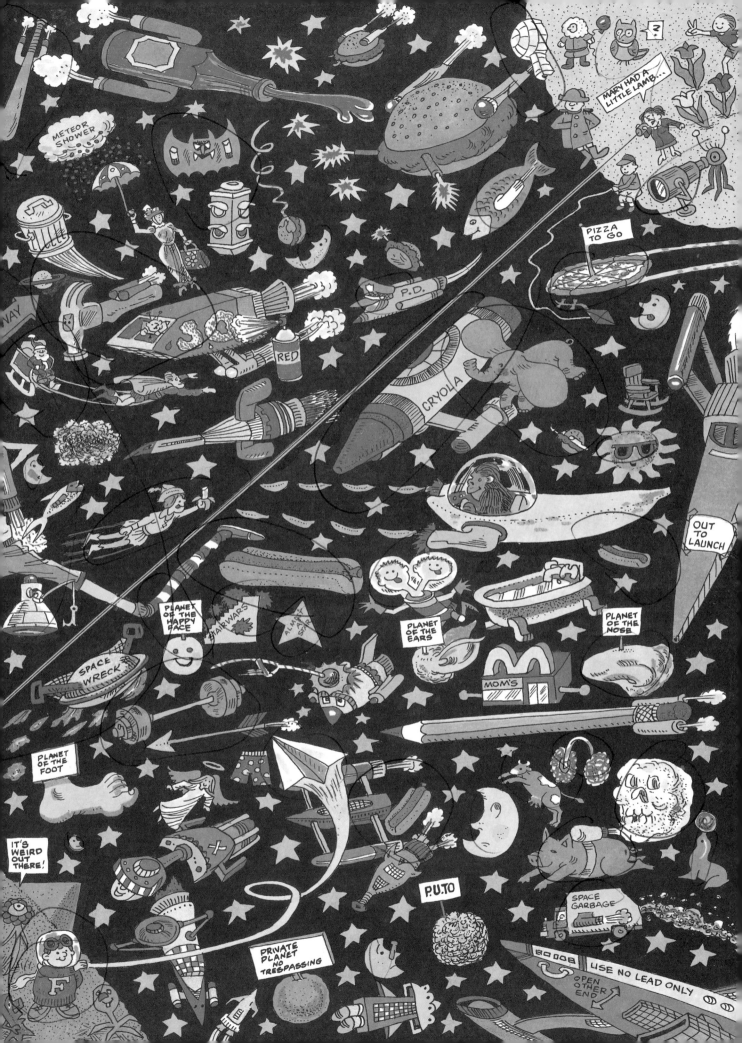

FIND FREDDIE AT THE BEACH AND ...

- ☑ Angry dog
- ☑ Angry horse
- ☑ Bulldozer
- ☑ Caddy
- ☑ Castle
- ☑ 3 Cats
- ☑ Eskimo
- ☑ Firefighter
- ☑ 3 Football players
- ☑ Hungry fish
- ☑ Hungry lion
- ☑ 2 Ice cream cones
- ☑ Kangaroo
- ☑ Launch site
- ☑ Laundry
- ☑ Life raft
- ☑ Mailbox
- ☑ Motorcyclist
- ☑ "New Sand"
- ☑ Octopus
- ☑ Oil well
- ☑ Paint-by-number
- ☑ Panda
- ☑ Periscope
- ☑ Policeman
- ☑ "Quicksand"
- ☑ 2 Radios
- ☑ Record
- ☑ Robot
- ☑ Rock surfer
- ☑ Seahorse
- ☑ Sea serpent
- ☑ Seltzer bottle
- ☑ Singing cowboy
- ☑ Snail
- ☑ Strong wind
- ☑ 3 Tires
- ☑ Tuba player
- ☑ 6 Turtles
- ☑ Twin boys
- ☑ 8 Umbrellas
- ☑ "Used Sand"
- ☑ Very fat man
- ☑ Wet dog

FIND FREDDIE AT SCHOOL AND...

- ☐ Apple
- ☐ Awakening monster
- ☐ Balloon
- ☐ "Ban Homework"
- ☐ Bare feet
- ☐ 2 Baseball bats
- ☐ Baton twirler
- ☐ Bowling ball
- ☐ Boy Scout
- ☐ Cake
- ☐ Cannon
- ☐ Clock setter
- ☐ Coach
- ☐ Cook
- ☐ "Disco"
- ☐ Explosion
- ☐ Fish tank
- ☐ Guitar
- ☐ Headless horseman
- ☐ Helium filled bubble gum
- ☐ Jump rope
- ☐ Lost ear
- ☐ Mouse attack
- ☐ Pumpkin
- ☐ 2 Rabbits
- ☐ 5 Report cards
- ☐ Roller skates
- ☐ Robot
- ☐ Rocket launch
- ☐ "Room To Let"
- ☐ 4 "School Closed" signs
- ☐ Secret trap door
- ☐ Ship
- ☐ 2 Sleeping students
- ☐ Snake
- ☐ Soccer practice
- ☐ Surfboard
- ☐ Tent
- ☐ Tuba
- ☐ 4 TV antennae
- ☐ Tyrannosaurus
- ☐ Water bomb
- ☐ Weightlifter

FIND FREDDIE ON THE SCHOOL BUS TRIP AND . . .

- ☐ Airplane
- ☐ Alligator
- ☐ Ambulance
- ☐ 5 Balloons
- ☐ Banana
- ☐ Barbershop
- ☐ Birdcage
- ☐ Boat
- ☐ "Bubble Gum Co."
- ☐ Burger-mobile
- ☐ Circus tent
- ☐ 3 Clocks
- ☐ Closed road
- ☐ Covered wagon
- ☐ Diver
- ☐ Doghouse
- ☐ Donkey
- ☐ Fish-mobile
- ☐ Garbage truck
- ☐ Gas station
- ☐ Ghost
- ☐ Horseshoe
- ☐ Hotel
- ☐ Igloo-mobile
- ☐ Jack-in-the-box
- ☐ Jellybean factory
- ☐ Lake serpent
- ☐ Library
- ☐ Locomotive
- ☐ 2 Mice
- ☐ Milk truck
- ☐ One-eyed monster
- ☐ Sailor cap
- ☐ Sandwich
- ☐ "72"
- ☐ 4 Sheep
- ☐ "Shopping Mall"
- ☐ 2 Skulls
- ☐ Sombrero
- ☐ Teepee-mobile
- ☐ Telephone
- ☐ Telescope
- ☐ Tennis racket
- ☐ Tow truck
- ☐ 2 Used tires

FIND FREDDIE IN MONSTERVILLE AND . . .

- ☐ 6 Arrows
- ☐ Bathbrush
- ☐ 13 Bats
- ☐ Ben Franklin
- ☐ Broken clock
- ☐ Broken heart
- ☐ Carrot
- ☐ Clothespin
- ☐ Cowgirl
- ☐ Daisy
- ☐ "Dead End"
- ☐ Dog
- ☐ Eye in the sky
- ☐ Flying carpet
- ☐ Garbage can
- ☐ 6 Ghosts
- ☐ "Harvard Drop-Out"
- ☐ Humpty Dumpty
- ☐ Ice cream cone
- ☐ Key
- ☐ "Kids Ahead"
- ☐ Kite
- ☐ Ladder
- ☐ Mailbox
- ☐ Mail carrier
- ☐ Ms. Transylvania
- ☐ "No Fishing"
- ☐ 3 Number 13's
- ☐ One-eyed monster
- ☐ "One way"
- ☐ Octopus
- ☐ 7 Pumpkins
- ☐ Rabbit
- ☐ Skeleton
- ☐ 8 Skulls
- ☐ Sprinkler
- ☐ Tic-tac-toe
- ☐ Truck
- ☐ TV set
- ☐ Weird doctor
- ☐ 2 Welcome mats
- ☐ Window washer
- ☐ Witch
- ☐ Young Dracula's wagon

FIND FREDDIE AT THE AIRPORT AND . . .

- ☐ Arrow
- ☐ Banana peel
- ☐ 3 Bats
- ☐ Bear
- ☐ Bird in love
- ☐ Boots
- ☐ Bride and groom
- ☐ Chicken
- ☐ Clown
- ☐ Cow
- ☐ Dart
- ☐ Dog pilot
- ☐ "Don't Fly"
- ☐ "Fly"
- ☐ Flying saucer
- ☐ 4 Fuel trucks
- ☐ Globe
- ☐ Golfer
- ☐ Hockey stick
- ☐ Horse
- ☐ "ICU2"
- ☐ Leaping lizard
- ☐ Long beard
- ☐ Luggage carrier
- ☐ "One Way"
- ☐ 3 Paper planes
- ☐ Photographer
- ☐ Pterosaur
- ☐ Rabbit
- ☐ 2 Sailboats
- ☐ Santa Claus
- ☐ Seesaw
- ☐ Sherlock Holmes
- ☐ Shooting star
- ☐ Space capsule
- ☐ "Star Wreck"
- ☐ Super hero
- ☐ Telescope
- ☐ Teepee
- ☐ 2 Unicorns
- ☐ Walnut
- ☐ Watermelon slice
- ☐ Windsock
- ☐ Winged man
- ☐ Wooden leg

FIND FREDDIE AT THE BALLPARK AND . . .

- ☐ Basketball
- ☐ 3 Beach balls
- ☐ 3 Birds
- ☐ Bone
- ☐ Boxing glove
- ☐ Bubble gum bubble
- ☐ Car
- ☐ Clothesline
- ☐ Cyclist
- ☐ 3 Dancers
- ☐ Elephant
- ☐ Fish
- ☐ Football team
- ☐ Frankenstein monster
- ☐ Ghost
- ☐ Giraffe
- ☐ Gorilla
- ☐ "Happy Section"
- ☐ 3 Hearts
- ☐ Horse
- ☐ 2 "Hot" dogs
- ☐ Lawn mower
- ☐ Lost shoe
- ☐ Mascot
- ☐ Monster hand
- ☐ 6 "No. 1" hands
- ☐ "Out" banner
- ☐ Painter
- ☐ 5 Paper airplanes
- ☐ Parachutist
- ☐ Rabbit
- ☐ Showers
- ☐ Sleeping player
- ☐ Snowman
- ☐ Tic-tac-toe
- ☐ Torn pants
- ☐ Turtle
- ☐ 4 TV cameras
- ☐ 2 TV sets
- ☐ Two-gloved fan
- ☐ 3 Umbrellas
- ☐ Uncle Sam
- ☐ Viking
- ☐ Yellow slicker

FIND FREDDIE AT THE MUSEUM AND . . .

- ☐ 4 Artists
- ☐ Baby crying
- ☐ 3 Bees
- ☐ Bike racer
- ☐ Bomb
- ☐ Bowler
- ☐ Boy Scout
- ☐ Cactus
- ☐ Doctor
- ☐ Dracula
- ☐ Elephant
- ☐ Escaped convict
- ☐ Fire hose
- ☐ "First Prize"
- ☐ Girl fishing
- ☐ "For Sail"
- ☐ Giant soda
- ☐ Giant whistle
- ☐ Hamburger
- ☐ Hammock
- ☐ 5 Hearts
- ☐ Jester
- ☐ Juggler
- ☐ "Last Clean Air"
- ☐ Man rowing
- ☐ Mirror
- ☐ Mummy
- ☐ Musician
- ☐ Peanuts
- ☐ Peanut vendor
- ☐ Photographer
- ☐ Pizza delivery
- ☐ Princess
- ☐ Rope climber
- ☐ Sand castle
- ☐ Santa Claus
- ☐ Sherlock Holmes
- ☐ "Slowsand"
- ☐ Smoke signals
- ☐ Space capsule
- ☐ Sun
- ☐ Target
- ☐ Taxi
- ☐ Telephone booth
- ☐ "Thin Ice"

FIND FREDDIE IN THE OLD WEST TOWN AND . . .

- [ ] Alien
- [ ] Bald Indian
- [ ] Banana peel
- [ ] Bearded man
- [ ] 7 Bedbugs
- [ ] Boot Hill
- [ ] 6 Cactuses
- [ ] Cat
- [ ] "Condos"
- [ ] 5 Ducklings
- [ ] Fire hydrant
- [ ] Fistfight
- [ ] Flying saucer
- [ ] "Ghost Town"
- [ ] Hand-in-a-box
- [ ] Hobo hitchhiker
- [ ] Jailbreak
- [ ] Jockey
- [ ] Lasso
- [ ] Long johns
- [ ] One-man-band
- [ ] Painted mountain
- [ ] Parking meter
- [ ] Piano player
- [ ] Piggy bank
- [ ] 3 Rabbits
- [ ] Rain cloud
- [ ] Rhinoceros
- [ ] Rocking horse
- [ ] Satellite dish
- [ ] Shark fin
- [ ] Sharpshooter
- [ ] Sheriff
- [ ] Snake
- [ ] Snowman
- [ ] Soccer ball
- [ ] Stampede
- [ ] "Tacos"
- [ ] 8 Teepees
- [ ] "Texas"
- [ ] Theater
- [ ] 2 Tombstones
- [ ] Unicorn
- [ ] Witch

FIND FREDDIE

LOOK FOR LISA

HUNT FOR HECTOR

SEARCH FOR SAM

HUNT FOR HECTOR

WHERE ARE THEY?

Where's Hector?
You'll have to search through these
wacky scenes—and more—to find him!

- Cats at the Dog Mall
- K-9 secret agents
- Fencing dogs at the Olympics
- Fire hydrants in Dogtown
- Bones at the Hall of Fame
- Dancing dogs at school
- Hot dogs in space

. . . and lots more!

HUNT FOR HECTOR AT THE DOG HALL OF FAME AND . . .

- ☐ Alien
- ☐ Astronaut
- ☐ Automobile
- ☐ Babe Ruff
- ☐ 2 Birds
- ☐ Boot
- ☐ "Buffalo Bull"
- ☐ Cannon
- ☐ Cat
- ☐ "Cave Dog"
- ☐ Clown
- ☐ Cook
- ☐ Doghouse
- ☐ "Down Boy"
- ☐ Elephant
- ☐ Fallen star
- ☐ Flying dog
- ☐ Football
- ☐ Ghost dog
- ☐ 2 Giant bones
- ☐ Guard dog
- ☐ Hot dog
- ☐ Husky
- ☐ Indian
- ☐ Juggler
- ☐ Kangaroo
- ☐ Man on leash
- ☐ Mirror
- ☐ Moon
- ☐ Mouse
- ☐ Napoleon
- ☐ Photographer
- ☐ Pilgrim
- ☐ Pirate flag
- ☐ Record player
- ☐ Santa hound
- ☐ Sheep
- ☐ Sherlock Bones
- ☐ Stamp
- ☐ Super hero
- ☐ Super poodle
- ☐ Target
- ☐ Tin can
- ☐ Umpire

HUNT FOR HECTOR AT DOG SCHOOL AND . . .

- ☐ A-ARF
- ☐ Artist's model
- ☐ Banana peel
- ☐ Building plans
- ☐ Cat
- ☐ Chalk
- ☐ Clipboard
- ☐ Cloud
- ☐ Comic book
- ☐ Cook
- ☐ Cork
- ☐ Crown
- ☐ 2 Dancing dogs
- ☐ Doggy bag
- ☐ Doggy bank
- ☐ Dogwood
- ☐ Dunce cap
- ☐ Eraser
- ☐ Fire hydrant
- ☐ Flying bone
- ☐ 2 Forks
- ☐ Frankendog
- ☐ Genie
- ☐ Graduate
- ☐ Hammer
- ☐ Handkerchief
- ☐ "Hi, Mom!"
- ☐ "History Of Bones"
- ☐ Hockey stick
- ☐ "How To Bark"
- ☐ Leash
- ☐ Mail carrier
- ☐ Mush
- ☐ 2 Pencils
- ☐ P.T.A.
- ☐ Roller skates
- ☐ Saw
- ☐ 2 School bags
- ☐ Scooter
- ☐ Sun
- ☐ Sunglasses
- ☐ Triangle
- ☐ T-square

HUNT FOR HECTOR
AMONG THE DOG
CATCHERS
AND . . .

- ☐ Airplane
- ☐ Alien
- ☐ "Arf"
- ☐ Balloon
- ☐ Barber pole
- ☐ Carrots
- ☐ 5 Cats
- ☐ 3 Chimneys
- ☐ 3 Dog bowls
- ☐ 7 Dog catchers
- ☐ Doghouse
- ☐ Drums
- ☐ Firedogs
- ☐ 4 Fire hydrants
- ☐ Fisherdog
- ☐ 2 Flagpoles
- ☐ Flying saucer
- ☐ Gas mask
- ☐ 2 Howling dogs
- ☐ "Keep Things Clean"
- ☐ Mailbox
- ☐ Manhole cover
- ☐ 9 Police dogs
- ☐ 2 Restaurants
- ☐ Roadblock
- ☐ Rock and roll dog
- ☐ Santa dog
- ☐ Scout
- ☐ Shower
- ☐ Slice of pizza
- ☐ Streetlight
- ☐ 4 Super hero dogs
- ☐ Telephone
- ☐ Trail of money
- ☐ Trash can
- ☐ Tree
- ☐ 10 Trucks
- ☐ Turtle
- ☐ TV antenna
- ☐ TV camera
- ☐ Umbrella

HUNT FOR HECTOR
WHERE THE RICH
AND FAMOUS DOGS
LIVE AND . . .

- ☐ Admiral
- ☐ Alligator
- ☐ Artist
- ☐ Bank
- ☐ "Big Wheel"
- ☐ Bird bath
- ☐ Blimp
- ☐ Bone chimney
- ☐ Candle
- ☐ Castle
- ☐ Cat
- ☐ 2 Cooks
- ☐ Crown
- ☐ Dog fish
- ☐ Dog flag
- ☐ Dog prince statue
- ☐ 2 Dog-shaped bushes
- ☐ Door dog
- ☐ Fat dog
- ☐ Fire hydrant
- ☐ Fisherdog's catch
- ☐ 2 Golfers
- ☐ Guard
- ☐ Heart
- ☐ Heron
- ☐ High rise condos
- ☐ Human
- ☐ 3 Joggers
- ☐ 6 Limousines
- ☐ Periscope
- ☐ Pillow
- ☐ Pool
- ☐ Sipping a soda
- ☐ Star
- ☐ Tennis player
- ☐ TV antenna
- ☐ Umbrella
- ☐ Violinist
- ☐ Water-skier
- ☐ Whale

HUNT FOR HECTOR AT THE K-9 CLEANUP AND . . .

- ☐ Anchor
- ☐ Bath brush
- ☐ 3 Birds
- ☐ Bomb
- ☐ Broom
- ☐ 2 Burned out light bulbs
- ☐ Cannon
- ☐ Cat
- ☐ Coffin
- ☐ Dog bowl
- ☐ Doghouse
- ☐ Dog in disguise
- ☐ Elephant
- ☐ 4 Empty food cans
- ☐ 3 Fire hydrants
- ☐ Fire pig
- ☐ Fisherdog
- ☐ Flying fish
- ☐ Frankenswine
- ☐ Garbage can
- ☐ Horse
- ☐ Indian dog
- ☐ "K-8"
- ☐ Life preserver
- ☐ Lunch box
- ☐ Mermaid
- ☐ Mob spy
- ☐ Mouse
- ☐ Net
- ☐ Oil leak
- ☐ Old dog
- ☐ Old tire
- ☐ Palm tree
- ☐ Penguin
- ☐ Periscope
- ☐ Pighole cover
- ☐ Rabbit
- ☐ Rubber duck
- ☐ Sailor pig
- ☐ Skateboard
- ☐ Telescope
- ☐ Violin case

HUNT FOR HECTOR AT THE SUPER DOG BOWL AND . . .

- ☐ "Almost Wet Paint"
- ☐ Arrow
- ☐ Beach ball
- ☐ Bird
- ☐ Bowling ball
- ☐ Cactus
- ☐ Candycane
- ☐ Cheerleaders
- ☐ Chicken
- ☐ Coach
- ☐ "Dog Aid"
- ☐ "Dogs U"
- ☐ Egg
- ☐ "Exit"
- ☐ 3 Flowers
- ☐ Ghost
- ☐ Heart
- ☐ Hobby horse
- ☐ Hot dog
- ☐ Megaphone
- ☐ "Mom"
- ☐ Mouse
- ☐ "No Barking"
- ☐ "Number 1"
- ☐ Paddleball
- ☐ Paintbrush
- ☐ 2 Pigs
- ☐ Pirate
- ☐ Propeller cap
- ☐ 5 Pumpkins
- ☐ Rabbit
- ☐ Skull and crossbones
- ☐ Super Bowl I
- ☐ Super Bowl II
- ☐ Super Bowl III
- ☐ Sword
- ☐ Tombstone
- ☐ Turtle
- ☐ TV camera
- ☐ TV set
- ☐ Water bucket
- ☐ "Wet Paint"
- ☐ Worm

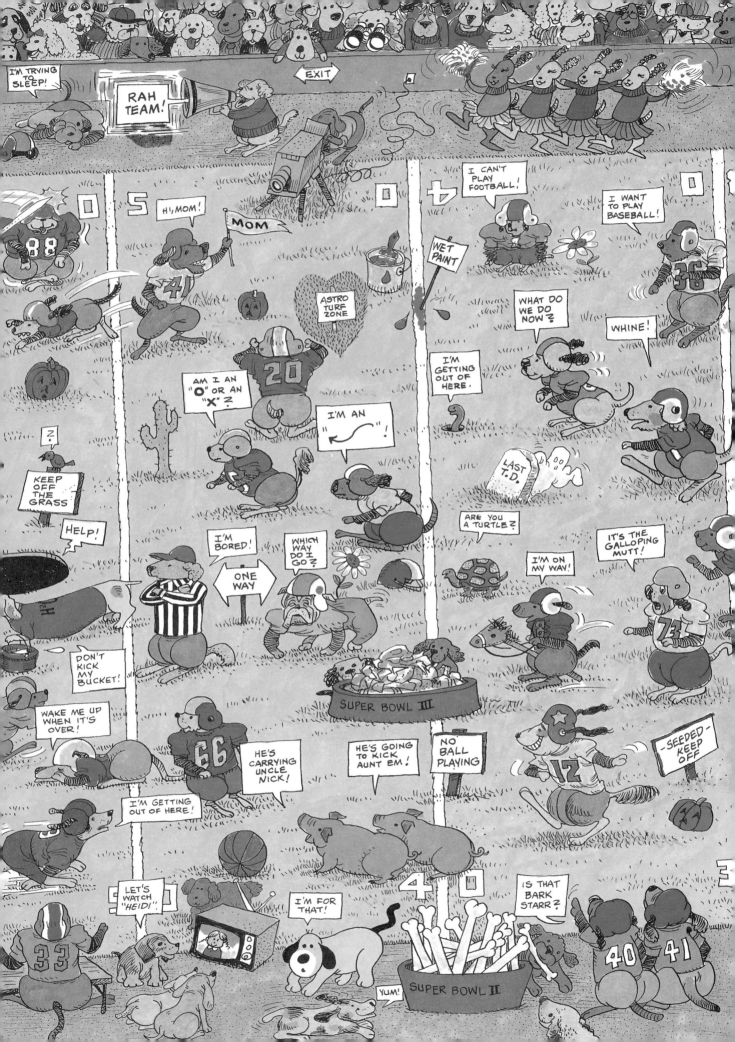

HUNT FOR HECTOR AT THE DOG MALL AND . . .

- ☐ Ball
- ☐ Balloon
- ☐ Barber shop
- ☐ Bat
- ☐ Bird's house
- ☐ Candle
- ☐ Candy cane
- ☐ 2 Cats
- ☐ Cheerleader
- ☐ Clown
- ☐ 2 Cookies
- ☐ Cup
- ☐ Dog bowls "Sale"
- ☐ Dog cake
- ☐ Doghouse
- ☐ Fish
- ☐ Flamingo
- ☐ Ghost
- ☐ Headphones
- ☐ Heart
- ☐ Helmet
- ☐ Howling Dog
- ☐ Human
- ☐ Ice cream cone
- ☐ Knight in armor
- ☐ Lollipop
- ☐ Mask
- ☐ Mouse
- ☐ Newsdog
- ☐ Newspaper reader
- ☐ Nut
- ☐ Paper airplane
- ☐ Pelican
- ☐ Pizza slice
- ☐ Police dog
- ☐ Pumpkin
- ☐ Scarf
- ☐ Stool
- ☐ Sunglasses
- ☐ Tennis racket
- ☐ Tire
- ☐ 2 Trash baskets
- ☐ Trophy
- ☐ Waiter

HUNT FOR HECTOR AT THE DOG OLYMPICS AND . . .

- ☐ Archer
- ☐ 7 Arrows
- ☐ Basketball
- ☐ Batter
- ☐ Bomb
- ☐ Bone balloon
- ☐ Boomerang
- ☐ Broom
- ☐ Caddy
- ☐ Car chase
- ☐ Cyclers
- ☐ Dunce cap
- ☐ Fencers
- ☐ "Fetch"
- ☐ Football
- ☐ "Go Dogs"
- ☐ Golf ball
- ☐ Gymnasts
- ☐ "Hi, Mom"
- ☐ Hockey game
- ☐ Horse
- ☐ Horseshoe
- ☐ Ice cream cone
- ☐ Karate chop
- ☐ Lacrosse stick
- ☐ Paper plane
- ☐ Pole vaulter
- ☐ Rower
- ☐ Skateboard
- ☐ Skier
- ☐ 2 Sleeping dogs
- ☐ Snow dog
- ☐ Soccer ball
- ☐ Starter's gun
- ☐ "Stop"
- ☐ Target
- ☐ Trainer
- ☐ TV camera
- ☐ "Very Thin Ice"
- ☐ Weight lifter
- ☐ Yo-yo

HUNT FOR HECTOR
AT THE TV QUIZ
SHOW
AND . . .

- ☐ "Answer"
- ☐ Ape
- ☐ Astronaut
- ☐ Band
- ☐ Binoculars
- ☐ 2 Birds
- ☐ Candle
- ☐ Cap
- ☐ Cue cards
- ☐ Director
- ☐ Elephant
- ☐ Fairy dog
- ☐ Fire hydrant
- ☐ Flashlight
- ☐ Flowerpot
- ☐ Giant dog bowl
- ☐ Giraffe
- ☐ Gold bar
- ☐ Hot dogs
- ☐ "Howl"
- ☐ "Junk Food"
- ☐ King dog
- ☐ Leash
- ☐ "Let's Go Dogs"
- ☐ Lunch box
- ☐ 4 Microphones
- ☐ Mouse
- ☐ Oil can
- ☐ Party hat
- ☐ Pearls
- ☐ Photographer
- ☐ "Quiet"
- ☐ Ring
- ☐ Robot
- ☐ Sleeping dog
- ☐ Snowman
- ☐ Sock
- ☐ Steak
- ☐ Straw hat
- ☐ "Take 1"
- ☐ 5 TV cameras
- ☐ TV set
- ☐ "V.I.P. Room"

HUNT FOR HECTOR IN SPACE AND . . .

- ☐ Bark Vader
- ☐ Boat
- ☐ Boney Way
- ☐ Book
- ☐ Bow-wow land
- ☐ Boxing glove
- ☐ Cat
- ☐ Condo
- ☐ Dog catcher
- ☐ Dog graduate
- ☐ Dog trek
- ☐ Doggy bag
- ☐ Duck Rogers
- ☐ Emergency stop
- ☐ Fire hydrant
- ☐ Flying dog house
- ☐ Flying food dish
- ☐ Jail
- ☐ Kite
- ☐ Launch site
- ☐ Lost and found
- ☐ Mail carrier
- ☐ Map
- ☐ Moon dog
- ☐ "No Barking"
- ☐ Parachute
- ☐ Pirate
- ☐ Pizza
- ☐ Planet of the bones
- ☐ Planet of the dogs
- ☐ Police dog
- ☐ Pup tent
- ☐ Puppy trainer
- ☐ Robot dog
- ☐ Sleeping dog
- ☐ Space circus
- ☐ Surfboard
- ☐ Swimming pool
- ☐ Tire
- ☐ Unicycle
- ☐ Vampire dog
- ☐ Vanishing dog

HUNT FOR HECTOR IN DOGTOWN AND . . .

- ☐ "The Arf Building"
- ☐ Barbecue
- ☐ Bird bath
- ☐ Boat
- ☐ Bone crop
- ☐ Bookstore
- ☐ 2 Broken clocks
- ☐ 8 Broken windows
- ☐ 2 Cats
- ☐ "Curb Your Human"
- ☐ Dance studio
- ☐ 5 Fire hydrants
- ☐ Flag
- ☐ "For Rent"
- ☐ Fountain
- ☐ "Frozen Dog Food"
- ☐ Gas station
- ☐ "Happy Dog Mush"
- ☐ 3 Hard hats
- ☐ Ice cream truck
- ☐ Jogger
- ☐ Lawn mower
- ☐ Mail carrier
- ☐ Mechanic
- ☐ Motorcycle
- ☐ Movie theater
- ☐ Newsdog
- ☐ "People Catcher"
- ☐ Piano
- ☐ Pool
- ☐ Santa Claus
- ☐ Sleigh
- ☐ Sock
- ☐ Video shop
- ☐ Wagon
- ☐ Water tower
- ☐ Weather vane
- ☐ Window washer

HUNT FOR HECTOR   SEARCH FOR SAM   FIND FREDDIE   LOOK FOR LISA

LOOK FOR LISA

WHERE ARE THEY?

Look for Lisa in all sorts of crazy places!
While you're looking,`
you'll see crazy things, such as:

- Hippos at a rock concert
- Cactuses on the beach
- Parrots in the library
- Surfers on a farm
- Frogs at the flea market
- Snow White at the marathon
- Unicorns in Utah

. . . and much, much more!

LOOK FOR LISA
AT THE MARATHON
AND . . .

- ☐ Alien
- ☐ Alligator
- ☐ Ape
- ☐ Astronaut
- ☐ 2 Banana peels
- ☐ Barbell
- ☐ 5 Bats
- ☐ Big nose
- ☐ Cable car
- ☐ Cake
- ☐ Caveman
- ☐ 8 Chimneys
- ☐ Clown
- ☐ Convict
- ☐ Deep sea diver
- ☐ Drummer
- ☐ 2 Elephants
- ☐ Fire fighter
- ☐ Fish
- ☐ Flying carpet
- ☐ Football player
- ☐ Frankenstein monster
- ☐ Horse
- ☐ Ice skater
- ☐ Long-haired lady
- ☐ Man in a barrel
- ☐ Moose head
- ☐ Octopus
- ☐ Pig
- ☐ 6 Quitters
- ☐ Santa Claus
- ☐ Skier
- ☐ Sleeping jogger
- ☐ Snow White
- ☐ Tuba
- ☐ 2 Turtles
- ☐ Vampire
- ☐ Viking
- ☐ Waiter
- ☐ Worm

LOOK FOR LISA AFTER SCHOOL AND . . .

- ☐ Airplane
- ☐ 2 Aliens
- ☐ Beanie with propeller
- ☐ Beard
- ☐ Blackboard
- ☐ Books on wheels
- ☐ Bucket
- ☐ Bus driver
- ☐ "Class brain"
- ☐ Clown
- ☐ Coach
- ☐ Dog
- ☐ Fire hydrant
- ☐ Football player
- ☐ Ghost
- ☐ Hockey player
- ☐ "Junior"
- ☐ Man trapped in a book
- ☐ 3 Mice
- ☐ Monkey
- ☐ Periscope
- ☐ Photographer
- ☐ Piano player
- ☐ Pillow
- ☐ "P.U."
- ☐ Pumpkin
- ☐ Radio
- ☐ Sailor
- ☐ School mascot
- ☐ Scooter
- ☐ Shopping cart
- ☐ Skateboard
- ☐ Ski jumper
- ☐ Socks
- ☐ Sports car
- ☐ Sunglasses
- ☐ Tepee
- ☐ Top hat
- ☐ Trash basket
- ☐ Unicorn
- ☐ Wagon

LOOK FOR LISA
AT THE ROCK
CONCERT AND . . .

- [ ] Alligator
- [ ] Apple
- [ ] Artist
- [ ] Beans
- [ ] Clown
- [ ] 2 Dogs
- [ ] Dwarf
- [ ] "Empty TV"
- [ ] Farmer
- [ ] Football player
- [ ] 4 Ghosts
- [ ] Giraffe
- [ ] 3 Guitars
- [ ] Heart
- [ ] 2 Hippos
- [ ] Hot dogs
- [ ] Hot foot
- [ ] Jogger
- [ ] Lamppost
- [ ] Lost balloon
- [ ] Magician
- [ ] "No Bus Stop"
- [ ] Pig
- [ ] Pink flamingo
- [ ] Pizza delivery
- [ ] Real cross wind
- [ ] Record albums
- [ ] Robot
- [ ] Rock
- [ ] Rock queen
- [ ] Roll
- [ ] Rooster
- [ ] Scarecrow
- [ ] School bus
- [ ] Skateboard
- [ ] 15 Speakers
- [ ] Stars
- [ ] Tent
- [ ] "Too Heavy
  Metal"
- [ ] Turtle
- [ ] Witch
- [ ] Zebra

LOOK FOR LISA ON THE FARM AND . . .

- ☐ Ax
- ☐ Basketball hoop
- ☐ Birdbath
- ☐ Bubble gum
- ☐ 4 Chickens
- ☐ Covered wagon
- ☐ 2 Cows
- ☐ Dart board
- ☐ Deer
- ☐ 2 Ducks
- ☐ Flower bed
- ☐ Fox
- ☐ 3 Giant apples
- ☐ Giraffe
- ☐ Goat
- ☐ Haunted house
- ☐ Heart
- ☐ 3 Horses
- ☐ Igloo
- ☐ "Junk Food"
- ☐ 4 Kites
- ☐ Lion
- ☐ Milk containers
- ☐ 2 Monsters
- ☐ Mule
- ☐ Note in a bottle
- ☐ Piggy bank
- ☐ 2 Pigs
- ☐ Popcorn
- ☐ Rooster
- ☐ Satellite dish
- ☐ 5 Scarecrows
- ☐ Shark fin
- ☐ 2 Surfers
- ☐ Tractor
- ☐ Turkey
- ☐ Turtle
- ☐ TV antenna
- ☐ Used tire
- ☐ Well
- ☐ Worm

LOOK FOR LISA AT THE BEACH AND . . .

- ☐ Artist
- ☐ Barrel of pickles
- ☐ Birdbath
- ☐ Boot
- ☐ 3 Bottles with notes
- ☐ Bubble gum
- ☐ 4 Cactuses
- ☐ 2 Clowns
- ☐ Cow
- ☐ Crocodile
- ☐ Dart thrower
- ☐ 4 Flying fish
- ☐ Hammerhead shark
- ☐ Leaking boat
- ☐ Lifesaver
- ☐ Litterbug
- ☐ Lost bathing suit
- ☐ 3 Mermaids
- ☐ Motorcyclist
- ☐ Mummy
- ☐ Musician
- ☐ Oil rig
- ☐ Pirate ship
- ☐ Polluted area
- ☐ 3 Radios
- ☐ Robinson Crusoe
- ☐ Rowboat
- ☐ Sailfish
- ☐ Seahorse
- ☐ Sea serpent
- ☐ Sleeping man
- ☐ Skull cave
- ☐ Stingray
- ☐ Submarine
- ☐ 6 Surfboards
- ☐ Telescope
- ☐ Thief
- ☐ Tricyclist
- ☐ Very quick sand
- ☐ 2 Water skiers

LOOK FOR LISA AT THE BIG SALE AND . . .

- ☐ Bicycle built for two
- ☐ Book department
- ☐ Broken dish
- ☐ Carrot
- ☐ Cash register
- ☐ Chauffeur
- ☐ Earmuffs
- ☐ Elephant
- ☐ Fairy godmother
- ☐ Falling $
- ☐ 2 Fish
- ☐ Fishing pole
- ☐ Frying pan
- ☐ "1/2 off"
- ☐ Kite
- ☐ Ladder
- ☐ Man with sore feet
- ☐ Moose head
- ☐ Mouse
- ☐ Octopus
- ☐ Paint brush
- ☐ Paper plane
- ☐ Perfume counter
- ☐ Pogo stick
- ☐ Pole-vaulter
- ☐ Robot
- ☐ Rocket ship
- ☐ Rope climber
- ☐ Santa Claus
- ☐ Skier
- ☐ 2 Sleeping shoppers
- ☐ "Stale"
- ☐ Strange mirror
- ☐ Super hero
- ☐ Tall person
- ☐ Telescope
- ☐ Toy department
- ☐ Up and down escalator
- ☐ Vampire

LOOK FOR LISA AROUND THE WORLD AND . . .

- ☐ Bear
- ☐ Big foot
- ☐ 2 Bridge builders
- ☐ Cactus
- ☐ Camel
- ☐ Cowboy
- ☐ Cup of coffee
- ☐ Cup of tea
- ☐ Dog
- ☐ Eskimo
- ☐ 12 Fish
- ☐ 2 Flying saucers
- ☐ Golfer
- ☐ Heart
- ☐ Ice castle
- ☐ Igloo
- ☐ Kangaroo
- ☐ Lighthouse
- ☐ Lion
- ☐ Mermaid
- ☐ Merman
- ☐ Oil well
- ☐ Ox
- ☐ 6 Penguins
- ☐ Rock singer
- ☐ 4 Sailboats
- ☐ Sea serpent
- ☐ 4 Skiers
- ☐ 2 Snowmen
- ☐ Stuck ship
- ☐ Submarine
- ☐ 3 Surfers
- ☐ Telescope
- ☐ 6 "Travel Agent" signs
- ☐ Tug boat
- ☐ T.V. set
- ☐ Unicorns in Utah
- ☐ Viking ship
- ☐ Walrus
- ☐ Whale

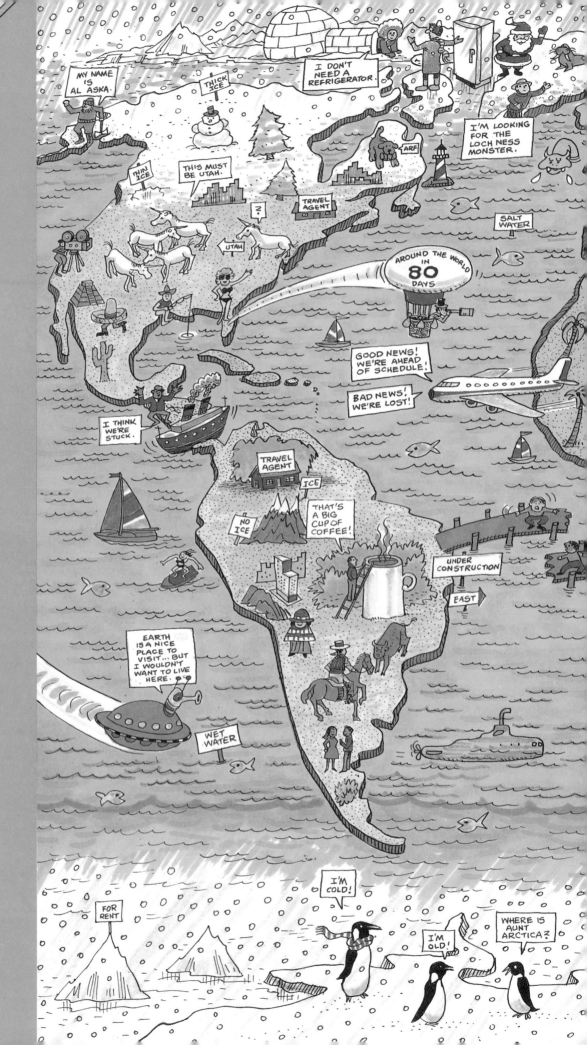

LOOK FOR LISA AT THE LIBRARY AND . . .

- ☐ Angel
- ☐ Banana peel
- ☐ Baseball cap
- ☐ Basketball players
- ☐ Book in a bottle
- ☐ 2 Bowling balls
- ☐ 4 Bullet holes
- ☐ Caveman
- ☐ Clown
- ☐ Copy machine
- ☐ 2 Cowboys
- ☐ Doctor
- ☐ Flying saucer
- ☐ Football
- ☐ Giant
- ☐ Hamburger
- ☐ Hammer
- ☐ Happy face
- ☐ 4 Hearts
- ☐ Hockey stick
- ☐ Horse
- ☐ Hula hoop
- ☐ Humpty Dumpty
- ☐ Moon
- ☐ Mummy and child
- ☐ Palm tree
- ☐ Paper plane
- ☐ 2 Parrots
- ☐ Pizza
- ☐ 7 "Quiet" signs
- ☐ 2 Radios
- ☐ Red wagon
- ☐ Referee
- ☐ Ship
- ☐ Skis
- ☐ 3 Skulls
- ☐ Telescope
- ☐ Tennis racket
- ☐ Tiny people
- ☐ TV camera
- ☐ Vacuum cleaner
- ☐ Worn tire

LOOK FOR LISA
AT THE
AMUSEMENT PARK
AND . . .

- [ ] Astronaut
- [ ] 15 Balloons
- [ ] Baseball
- [ ] Bomb
- [ ] Cactus
- [ ] Cheese
- [ ] Diplodocus
- [ ] "Do Not Read This"
- [ ] Entrance
- [ ] Exit
- [ ] Fishing hole
- [ ] 5 Ghosts
- [ ] Gorilla
- [ ] Graduate
- [ ] Headless man
- [ ] High diver
- [ ] Horse
- [ ] "Hot Dogs"
- [ ] "House Of Horrors"
- [ ] "Kisses"
- [ ] "Low Tide"
- [ ] 4 Mice
- [ ] 3 Monsters
- [ ] Mummy
- [ ] "No U-Turns"
- [ ] Pear
- [ ] Rocket
- [ ] Santa Claus
- [ ] "Scrambled Eggs"
- [ ] Skateboard
- [ ] Skull
- [ ] Snowman
- [ ] Thirteen o'clock
- [ ] Trash can
- [ ] Umbrella
- [ ] Vampire
- [ ] Witch

LOOK FOR LISA AT THE FLEA MARKET AND . . .

- ☐ Ape
- ☐ Bag of peanuts
- ☐ Baseball cards
- ☐ Bathtub
- ☐ Bicycle
- ☐ 2 Bird cages
- ☐ Box of records
- ☐ 2 Cactuses
- ☐ Candle
- ☐ Clown doll
- ☐ Cowboy
- ☐ 2 Dogs
- ☐ Duck
- ☐ 3 Fish
- ☐ Flower
- ☐ Football
- ☐ 2 Frogs
- ☐ Garbage basket
- ☐ Gas mask
- ☐ Giant shoe
- ☐ Graduate
- ☐ Hammer
- ☐ Knight in armor
- ☐ Lamp shade
- ☐ Man in bottle
- ☐ 2 Men with fleas
- ☐ Monster hand
- ☐ Pearl necklace
- ☐ Piggy bank
- ☐ Potted palm plant
- ☐ Rocking chair
- ☐ Saddle
- ☐ Scoutmaster
- ☐ Smoke signals
- ☐ Spinning wheel
- ☐ Sunglasses
- ☐ Tennis racket
- ☐ Toy locomotive
- ☐ Trumpet
- ☐ Yo-yo

LOOK FOR LISA
AS THE CIRCUS
COMES TO TOWN
AND . . .

- ☐ Ape
- ☐ Baby carriage
- ☐ 6 Balloons
- ☐ 2 Batons
- ☐ Bird
- ☐ Cactus
- ☐ Camel
- ☐ Candle
- ☐ Cannon
- ☐ Cat
- ☐ 13 Clowns
- ☐ 8 Dogs
- ☐ 5 Elephants
- ☐ "Exit"
- ☐ "For Rent"
- ☐ Giraffe
- ☐ 5 Happy faces
- ☐ 2 Indians
- ☐ Jack-in-the-box
- ☐ 2 Keystone cops
- ☐ Lion
- ☐ 2 Martians
- ☐ "Not Wet Paint"
- ☐ Rabbit
- ☐ Super hero
- ☐ 7 Tents
- ☐ Ticket seller
- ☐ Tightrope
  walker
- ☐ Tin man
- ☐ Top hat
- ☐ Turtle
- ☐ 3 Umbrellas
- ☐ Unicycle
- ☐ Weightlifter
- ☐ Witch

LOOK FOR LISA   FIND FREDDIE   SEARCH FOR SAM   HUNT FOR HECTOR

SEARCH FOR SAM

WHERE ARE THEY?

Sam's a sly cat, so good luck in your search!
You'll encounter hilarious characters in strange
scenes as you search for Sam.

- Dogs at the cat show
- Rhinos at the disco
- Alley cats in ancient Egypt
- Meows at midnight
- Fat cats at the gym
- Sharks in Cat City
- Dogbusters

. . . and lots more!

SEARCH FOR SAM IN CAT CITY AND . . .

- [ ] 2 Balloons
- [ ] Broken window
- [ ] Bus stop
- [ ] Car on sidewalk
- [ ] Catmobile
- [ ] Cat plane
- [ ] Clock
- [ ] Clown cat
- [ ] Cyclist
- [ ] "Do Not Litter"
- [ ] 2 Dogs
- [ ] Flat tire
- [ ] Flower pot
- [ ] Garbage truck
- [ ] 3 Ghost cats
- [ ] Human
- [ ] Ice skater
- [ ] Kite
- [ ] Kitty and Kats Avenues
- [ ] Locomotive
- [ ] 3 Mice
- [ ] Movie theater
- [ ] Penguin
- [ ] Piano
- [ ] Policecat
- [ ] Radio
- [ ] Roller skater
- [ ] Santa Claus
- [ ] Scarf
- [ ] 3 Sharks
- [ ] Ship on wheels
- [ ] 2 Skateboards
- [ ] Sleeping cat
- [ ] Sleigh
- [ ] Sock
- [ ] 5 Traffic accidents
- [ ] 8 Trash cans
- [ ] Waiter
- [ ] "What Time Is It?"
- [ ] Wind-up car

SEARCH FOR SAM
ON FRIDAY THE
13TH AND . . .

- [ ] Apple
- [ ] Ax
- [ ] Balloon
- [ ] 7 Bats
- [ ] 4 Black cats
- [ ] Bomb
- [ ] Candy cane
- [ ] Chicken
- [ ] Coffin
- [ ] Condos
- [ ] Cow
- [ ] Football
- [ ] "Ghost Office"
- [ ] 6 Ghosts
- [ ] Heart
- [ ] "Helping Hand"
- [ ] Junior vampire
- [ ] Kite eater
- [ ] Mad doctor
- [ ] Mailbox
- [ ] Man's head
- [ ] Mirror
- [ ] Mouse
- [ ] "No Screaming"
- [ ] Paint bucket
- [ ] Pirate
- [ ] 13 Pumpkins
- [ ] Quicksand
- [ ] Rabbit
- [ ] Ship
- [ ] Shovel
- [ ] Skull
- [ ] Snake
- [ ] 13 "13s"
- [ ] Trunk
- [ ] Turtle
- [ ] TV set
- [ ] Two-headed
  monster
- [ ] Vampire

SEARCH FOR SAM
AT THE FAT CAT
HEALTH CLUB
AND . . .

- [ ] Bird
- [ ] Bird cage
- [ ] Bone
- [ ] Bowling ball
- [ ] Broken chair
- [ ] 2 Cactus
- [ ] Daydream
- [ ] Dog
- [ ] Drumstick
- [ ] Dumbbells
- [ ] Escaped convict
- [ ] "Fat Is Beautiful!?"
- [ ] Fattest cat
- [ ] 2 Fish
- [ ] 6 Fish bones
- [ ] Fish bowl
- [ ] 4 Gym bags
- [ ] 3 Hearts
- [ ] 2 Ice cream cones
- [ ] Instructor
- [ ] Jump rope
- [ ] "Lose It!"
- [ ] 3 Mice
- [ ] 2 Milk containers
- [ ] Paper bag
- [ ] Pizza
- [ ] Quitter
- [ ] Roller skates
- [ ] Scratching post
- [ ] Sleeping cat
- [ ] Sore feet
- [ ] "Steam Room"
- [ ] 2 Stools
- [ ] Sunglasses
- [ ] Talking scale
- [ ] "Think Thin"
- [ ] Torn pants
- [ ] 4 Towels
- [ ] Wallet
- [ ] Woman

SEARCH FOR SAM AT THE MIDNIGHT MEOWING AND . . .

- ☐ Alarm clock
- ☐ 3 "Arf"
- ☐ 2 Birds
- ☐ Broken window
- ☐ 3 Brooms
- ☐ 7 Cannonballs
- ☐ "Cat Power!"
- ☐ Dog
- ☐ 2 Dog bones
- ☐ Dog dish
- ☐ Doll
- ☐ Egg
- ☐ 2 Fish bones
- ☐ Floor mat
- ☐ 3 Flower pots
- ☐ Ghost
- ☐ Hockey stick
- ☐ "Hush"
- ☐ "I like it!"
- ☐ Loudest screamer
- ☐ Microphone
- ☐ Mouse
- ☐ "No Meowing Zone"
- ☐ Open gate
- ☐ Phonograph
- ☐ Piggy bank
- ☐ Pillow
- ☐ Pumpkin
- ☐ Rhino
- ☐ Shoe
- ☐ Sleeping cat
- ☐ Slice of pizza
- ☐ Spaceship
- ☐ Stool
- ☐ Tin can
- ☐ Tire
- ☐ 4 Trash cans
- ☐ Witch
- ☐ Yo-yo

SEARCH FOR SAM AT THE DISCO AND . . .

- ☐ Ballerina
- ☐ 7 Balloons
- ☐ Break dancer
- ☐ Clown
- ☐ Cook
- ☐ Cowboy
- ☐ Dark glasses
- ☐ Disco duck
- ☐ Disco pig
- ☐ Dizzy cat
- ☐ Doctor
- ☐ Dog
- ☐ Duck
- ☐ Ear plugs
- ☐ Earrings
- ☐ Flower pot
- ☐ Hard hat
- ☐ Horn player
- ☐ Indian
- ☐ Karate cat
- ☐ Lamp shade
- ☐ 2 Mice
- ☐ Pig
- ☐ Pirate
- ☐ Pizza
- ☐ Police cat
- ☐ Rabbit
- ☐ Record eater
- ☐ Records
- ☐ 2 Rhinos
- ☐ Roller skates
- ☐ Scarf
- ☐ Skier
- ☐ Sleeping cat
- ☐ Snow cat
- ☐ 10 Speakers
- ☐ Swinging globe
- ☐ Top hat
- ☐ Record

SEARCH FOR SAM
AT THE BATTLE
OF CATS AND
MICE AND . . .

- ☐ Banana peel
- ☐ Baseball
- ☐ Big cheese
- ☐ "Catnip"
- ☐ Catapult
- ☐ Cheese donut
- ☐ Chimney mouse
- ☐ Clock
- ☐ Condo
- ☐ 2 Cream pies
- ☐ Cup
- ☐ Dog
- ☐ Drummer
- ☐ Fake mouse
- ☐ 3 Fish
- ☐ Flower
- ☐ 'Fraidy cat
- ☐ Frankencat
- ☐ 4 Hearts
- ☐ Hobby horse
- ☐ Horn blower
- ☐ Hose
- ☐ Ink
- ☐ Judge
- ☐ Key
- ☐ Knapsack
- ☐ Light bulb
- ☐ Mask
- ☐ Monkey
- ☐ Mouse trap
- ☐ Owl
- ☐ 2 Pigs
- ☐ Quill pen
- ☐ Sleeping mouse
- ☐ Spider
- ☐ Sword
- ☐ Top hat
- ☐ Watering can
- ☐ Worm
- ☐ Yarn

SEARCH FOR SAM
IN ANCIENT EGYPT
AND . . .

- ☐ Accident victim
- ☐ 2 Alley cats
- ☐ Bandit
- ☐ 4 Birds
- ☐ 4 Camels
- ☐ Cat kite
- ☐ "Catnip"
- ☐ Catopatra
- ☐ Crocodile
- ☐ Dog
- ☐ Dog house
- ☐ 2 Elephants
- ☐ 2 Falling
  coconuts
- ☐ Fan
- ☐ 3 Fish
- ☐ Flower
- ☐ Flying carpet
- ☐ Garage
- ☐ Happy face
- ☐ Hippo
- ☐ Hot sand
- ☐ Jester
- ☐ Ladder
- ☐ 6 Mice
- ☐ Mummy
- ☐ Oasis
- ☐ 8 Pyramids
- ☐ Quicksand
- ☐ Sculptor
- ☐ Slow sand
- ☐ Snake-in-
  the-grass
- ☐ Snake-in-
  the-sand
- ☐ Snowman
- ☐ 5 Spears
- ☐ Sunglasses
- ☐ Surfer
- ☐ Taxi
- ☐ Telephone
- ☐ TV antenna
- ☐ Umbrella

SEARCH FOR SAM AT THE CAT SHOW AND . . .

- ☐ Banjo
- ☐ Beach chair
- ☐ Bird
- ☐ Black cat
- ☐ Cat costume
- ☐ Cat guard
- ☐ Cat in a hat
- ☐ Cat on a woman's head
- ☐ Clown
- ☐ Cow
- ☐ Curtain
- ☐ 2 Dogs
- ☐ Elephant
- ☐ Fat cat
- ☐ 2 Fish bowls
- ☐ Fishing pole
- ☐ Groucho cat
- ☐ Hobo cat
- ☐ Jogging cat
- ☐ 3 Judges
- ☐ Light bulb
- ☐ Lion
- ☐ "Moo Juice"
- ☐ Mouse
- ☐ Photographer
- ☐ Pizza
- ☐ Pool
- ☐ "Princess"
- ☐ Scaredy cat
- ☐ Scarf
- ☐ Scratching post
- ☐ Sombrero
- ☐ Sunglasses
- ☐ Telescope
- ☐ "The Real 1st Prize"
- ☐ Tombstone
- ☐ Trombone
- ☐ "Wanted" poster
- ☐ Witch

SEARCH FOR SAM WITH THE DOGBUSTERS AND . . .

- ☐ "Bark 1-642"
- ☐ "Baseball Cards"
- ☐ Binoculars
- ☐ Bird
- ☐ Boat
- ☐ "Brooklyn"
- ☐ Blimp
- ☐ Bomb
- ☐ Cage
- ☐ Clown
- ☐ Crash
- ☐ Crocodile
- ☐ Dog house
- ☐ Fire hydrant
- ☐ Fish tank
- ☐ Happy face
- ☐ Helicopter
- ☐ "Hideout For Rent"
- ☐ Hockey stick
- ☐ Horse
- ☐ Manhole
- ☐ Monster
- ☐ 2 Mice
- ☐ Net
- ☐ Periscope
- ☐ "Pizza"
- ☐ "Poison Ivy"
- ☐ Pumpkin
- ☐ "Quiet"
- ☐ Rabbit
- ☐ Robot
- ☐ Rope ladder
- ☐ Saddle
- ☐ Super hero
- ☐ Surfer
- ☐ Tank
- ☐ Taxi
- ☐ Tent
- ☐ Truck
- ☐ Used tire
- ☐ Witch

SEARCH FOR SAM AT THE NORTH POLE AND . . .

- ☐ Ball
- ☐ Bear
- ☐ 2 Birds
- ☐ 3 Candles
- ☐ 6 Candy canes
- ☐ Coal
- ☐ Drum
- ☐ Duck
- ☐ Fallen skater
- ☐ Fishing
- ☐ 2 Fires
- ☐ Globe
- ☐ Gloves
- ☐ Hammer
- ☐ Jack-in-the-box
- ☐ Kitty bank
- ☐ Lollypop
- ☐ Mailbox
- ☐ Miner
- ☐ "North Pole"
- ☐ Pie
- ☐ Pumpkin
- ☐ Rabbit
- ☐ Rocking horse
- ☐ Roller skater
- ☐ Skier
- ☐ Sleeping cat
- ☐ Sleeping mouse
- ☐ 3 Sleds
- ☐ Snowball thrower
- ☐ Star
- ☐ 2 Stockings
- ☐ Toy soldier
- ☐ Tree ornament
- ☐ Turtle
- ☐ T.V. antenna
- ☐ Wheelbarrow
- ☐ Wrapping paper
- ☐ 2 Wreaths
- ☐ 2 Zebras

SEARCH FOR SAM

FIND FREDDIE

HUNT FOR HECTOR

LOOK FOR LISA

DETECT DONALD

It was a dark and rainy night in Hollywood. Detective Donald had stopped to eat at his favorite diner.

DETECT DONALD AT THE CHEEZ-E DINER AND...

☐ Arrow
☐ Bat
☐ Bird
☐ Bow ties (3)
☐ Bowling ball
☐ Cactus
☐ Convict
☐ Cook
☐ Crown
☐ Dracula
☐ Dragon
☐ Eyeglasses (3)
☐ Fish
☐ Genie
☐ Ghost
☐ Guitar
☐ Heart
☐ Humpty Dumpty
☐ Jack-o'-lantern
☐ Mouse
☐ Pirate
☐ Rabbit
☐ Skull
☐ Stars (3)
☐ Super heroes
☐ Top hat
☐ Two-headed man
☐ Waitresses (2)
☐ Witch
☐ Wristwatch

When he stepped outside, he detected something strange going on. First he saw a large group of strange characters. Then....

...Detective Donald almost got run over by a horse and carriage! There were no cars or buses and people were wearing wigs and funny hats. Detective Donald thought he saw George Washington—but it couldn't be! He decided to investigate to find out what was going on.

DETECT DONALD IN COLONIAL AMERICA AND...

- ☐ Antenna
- ☐ Baseball
- ☐ Basket
- ☐ Bell
- ☐ Ben Franklin
- ☐ Betsy Ross
- ☐ Bone
- ☐ Broom
- ☐ Bucket
- ☐ Candles (2)
- ☐ Cannonballs (4)
- ☐ Cats (2)
- ☐ Chicken
- ☐ Clock
- ☐ Dogs (2)
- ☐ Drums (3)
- ☐ Duck
- ☐ Ear of corn
- ☐ Flower vase
- ☐ Horses (4)
- ☐ Kites (2)
- ☐ Lamppost
- ☐ Mouse
- ☐ One dollar bill
- ☐ Saw
- ☐ Shopping bag
- ☐ Spinning wheel
- ☐ TV set
- ☐ Wagons (2)
- ☐ Watering can

Suddenly, two knights on horseback carrying long lances went charging by. A king, queen, knights and maidens were watching a jousting tournament. *Where was he now?* wondered Detective Donald.

DETECT DONALD IN THE MIDDLE AGES AND...

☐ Alligator
☐ Balloons (2)
☐ Birds (2)
☐ Candy cane
☐ Dog
☐ Doorbell
☐ Fan
☐ Fish
☐ Hot dog
☐ Ice-cream cone
☐ Jack-o'-lantern
☐ Jester
☐ King
☐ Kite
☐ Musician
☐ Periscope
☐ Pig
☐ Pot
☐ Robin Hood
☐ Rose
☐ Santa Claus
☐ Skull
☐ Sock
☐ Stars (2)
☐ Target
☐ Toast
☐ Umpire
☐ Unicorn
☐ Vendor
☐ Wizard

After watching the tournament for awhile, Detective Donald walked through the castle...

...and into a room filled with laughter! There were lots of cartoon characters acting silly all around him. Things were getting stranger and stranger.

DETECT DONALD IN CARTOONLAND AND...

- ☐ Balloon
- ☐ Banana peel
- ☐ Baseball
- ☐ Beehive
- ☐ Book
- ☐ Brush
- ☐ Cars (2)
- ☐ Cheese
- ☐ Clothesline
- ☐ Fire hydrant
- ☐ Fish (2)
- ☐ Fishing pole
- ☐ Flower
- ☐ Ghost
- ☐ Golf club
- ☐ Hose
- ☐ Ice-cream cone
- ☐ Magnifying glass
- ☐ Net
- ☐ Owl
- ☐ Sandwich
- ☐ Soap
- ☐ Star
- ☐ Sunglasses (2)
- ☐ Super dude
- ☐ Train engine
- ☐ Turtle
- ☐ TV set
- ☐ Umbrella

As Detective Donald walked through a hole in the wall, he heard...

..."Ahoy mates, a landlubber!" It was a pirate ship, and pirates were dashing about with swords doing battle with anyone and everyone.

DETECT DONALD AT THE PIRATES' BATTLE AND...

- [ ] Basketball
- [ ] Birds (3)
- [ ] Broom
- [ ] Candle
- [ ] Cannonballs (4)
- [ ] Captain Hook
- [ ] Cat
- [ ] Cup
- [ ] Duck
- [ ] Fish
- [ ] Football
- [ ] Guitar
- [ ] Half moon
- [ ] Headless horseman
- [ ] Hearts (2)
- [ ] Hot dog
- [ ] Jack-o'-lantern
- [ ] Knight
- [ ] Mice (7)
- [ ] Mirror
- [ ] Piano
- [ ] Rooster
- [ ] Sailboat
- [ ] Snake
- [ ] Top hat
- [ ] Treasure chest
- [ ] Turtles (3)
- [ ] Watering can
- [ ] Wooden legs (3)
- [ ] Yellow brick road

Detective Donald thought it best to quickly move on.

What was happening? Detective Donald's surroundings began to change before his very eyes! Strange buildings and bizarre creatures replaced the pirates.

DETECT DONALD IN THE WORLD OF THE FUTURE AND...

- ☐ Baby carriage
- ☐ Bat
- ☐ Bottle
- ☐ Bow
- ☐ Clothespin
- ☐ Dog
- ☐ Flat tire
- ☐ Hammer
- ☐ Key
- ☐ Kite
- ☐ Ladder
- ☐ Little red riding creature
- ☐ Mailbox
- ☐ Parachute
- ☐ Pencil
- ☐ Phonograph record
- ☐ Pocket watch
- ☐ Red wagon
- ☐ Submarine sandwich
- ☐ Schoolbag
- ☐ Sled
- ☐ Snowman
- ☐ Straw
- ☐ Teeth
- ☐ Tree
- ☐ Two-headed creature
- ☐ Tepee
- ☐ Vacuum cleaner
- ☐ Witch

Out an exit he went, and into...

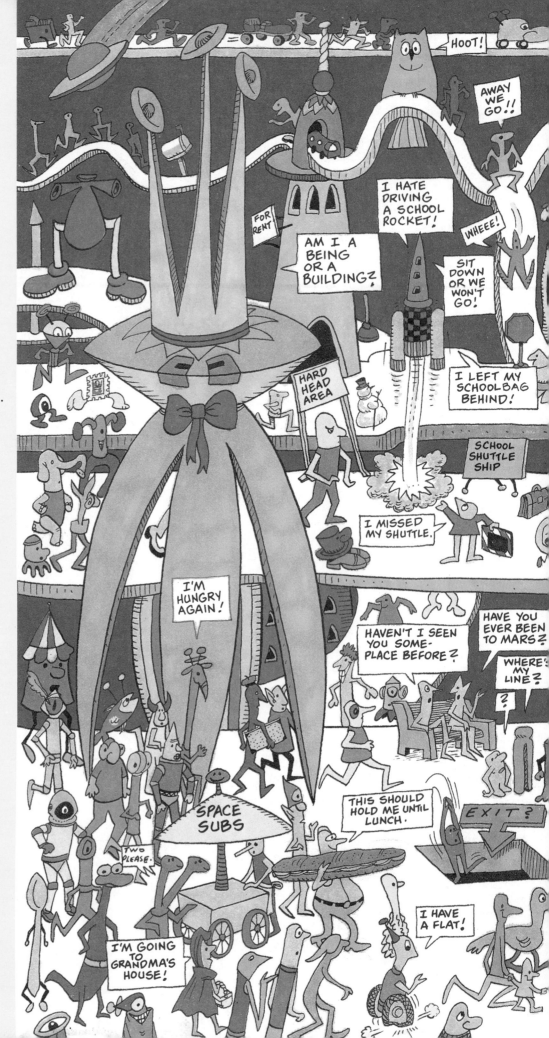

...French history a few hundred years ago. He was more confused than ever. Maybe I'm just having a weird dream, he thought.

DETECT DONALD IN NAPOLEON'S FRANCE AND...

- ☐ Alligator
- ☐ Axe
- ☐ Ballerina
- ☐ Balloon
- ☐ Baker
- ☐ Bell
- ☐ Cake
- ☐ Cannon
- ☐ Dracula
- ☐ Dragon
- ☐ Duck
- ☐ Eight ball
- ☐ Firecracker
- ☐ Flower
- ☐ French poodle
- ☐ King Kong
- ☐ Medals (2)
- ☐ Mermaid
- ☐ Movie camera
- ☐ Mummy
- ☐ Old tire
- ☐ One-eyed alien
- ☐ Pinocchio
- ☐ Radio
- ☐ Rapunzel
- ☐ Sailor
- ☐ Scarecrow
- ☐ Shark
- ☐ Tarzan
- ☐ Unicorn

Detective Donald kept searching and searching for clues. Next he found himself...

...in an army camp during basic training. Some soldiers were having fun, but most were happy when training was over. Detective Donald noticed a movie camera. Hmmm, he wondered, haven't I seen one somewhere before?

DETECT DONALD AT FORT KNOCKS AND...

☐ Ape
☐ Bat
☐ Bird
☐ Bodiless ghost
☐ Bombs (2)
☐ Cactus
☐ Chimneys (2)
☐ Cook
☐ Dunce cap
☐ Fan
☐ Fish (2)
☐ Jack-o'-lantern
☐ Lemonade stand
☐ Kite
☐ Medal
☐ Oil can
☐ Periscope
☐ Pitcher
☐ Pot
☐ Rat
☐ Robin Hood
☐ Sergeant's stripes (5)
☐ Skulls (2)
☐ Slingshot
☐ Snake
☐ Sock
☐ Traffic ticket
☐ Turtle
☐ Volcano

Donald walked past the chow line and into...

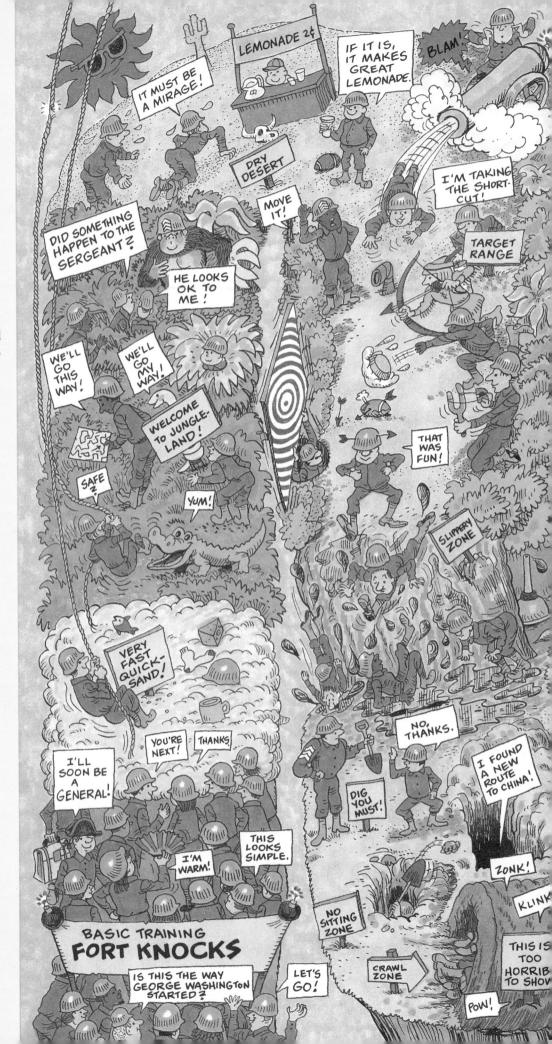

...the Roman Coliseum.
But it wasn't a ruin!
It was full of ancient
Romans rooting for or
against gladiators.

DETECT DONALD IN ANCIENT ROME AND...

- ☐ Abraham Lincoln
- ☐ Banana peel
- ☐ Bones (2)
- ☐ Boots
- ☐ Cheerleader
- ☐ Cleopatra
- ☐ Dog
- ☐ Dragons (2)
- ☐ Electric fan
- ☐ Elephant
- ☐ Football
- ☐ Giraffe
- ☐ Guitar
- ☐ Hot dog
- ☐ Hourglass
- ☐ Jester
- ☐ Kite
- ☐ Lions (3)
- ☐ Lunch boxes (2)
- ☐ Necktie
- ☐ Net
- ☐ Pig
- ☐ Raindrops (2)
- ☐ Red scarf
- ☐ Secret door
- ☐ Soccer ball
- ☐ Spears (2)
- ☐ Tin man
- ☐ Vendors (2)
- ☐ Watch
- ☐ Watering can

Detective Donald ducked
out behind the big
wooden horse and
immediately ran into...

...a wooly mammoth! It was huge and hairy, but how did it get here? Or, how did *he* get *there?* The spear-carrying cave people frightened Detective Donald so he leapt out of their way.

DETECT DONALD IN PREHISTORIC TIMES AND...

☐ Ape
☐ Arrow
☐ Baby bird
☐ Basketball
☐ Bicycle
☐ Bone
☐ Book
☐ Burglar
☐ Cannon
☐ Chef
☐ Clipboard
☐ Helmet
☐ Juggler
☐ Kettle
☐ Mailbox
☐ Nets (2)
☐ Periscope
☐ Pole-vaulter
☐ Rabbit
☐ Rocket
☐ Rocking chair
☐ Rocking horse
☐ Roller skates
☐ Skateboard
☐ Skier
☐ Tennis racket
☐ Toothbrush
☐ Tuba
☐ Turtle
☐ Umbrella
☐ Witch

Donald continued on until he came to the back of a curtain. He opened it in time to hear...

..."And now..." He was standing on a stage receiving an award! But why? Then a very embarrassed Detective Donald realized that, without knowing it, he had just walked through ten movie sets!

DETECT DONALD AT THE ACADEMY AWARDS AND...

- ☐ Aliens (2)
- ☐ Arrows (2)
- ☐ Baseball cap
- ☐ Bird
- ☐ "Boo" (2)
- ☐ Bowling ball
- ☐ Broken heart
- ☐ Candle
- ☐ Cook
- ☐ Darts (5)
- ☐ Dog
- ☐ Elephant
- ☐ Envelope
- ☐ Fish
- ☐ Flower
- ☐ Fork
- ☐ Ghost
- ☐ Half moon
- ☐ Heart
- ☐ Ice skates
- ☐ Lens cap
- ☐ Masks (2)
- ☐ Microphone
- ☐ Mushroom
- ☐ Pencil
- ☐ Rabbit
- ☐ Scarf
- ☐ Skulls (2)
- ☐ Snake
- ☐ Tomahawk

LOOK FOR LAURA   DETECT DONALD   FIND FRANKIE   SEARCH FOR SUSIE

FIND FRANKIE

It is the night of the Monster Club meeting. Every monster member, young and old, ugly and uglier is in attendance. The clubhouse is to be torn down and the monsters need a new place to meet. All the monsters are listening carefully—except Frankie.

FIND FRANKIE AT THE MONSTER CLUB MEETING AND...

- ☐ Arrow
- ☐ Ax
- ☐ Balloon
- ☐ Bats (4)
- ☐ Birdcage
- ☐ Bones (4)
- ☐ Broom
- ☐ Candles (7)
- ☐ Candy canes (2)
- ☐ Clothesline
- ☐ Cobweb
- ☐ Coffins (2)
- ☐ Cup
- ☐ Grapes
- ☐ Hot dog
- ☐ Jack-o'-lantern
- ☐ Mice (3)
- ☐ Nail
- ☐ Noose
- ☐ Pie
- ☐ Rabbit
- ☐ Skulls (4)
- ☐ Teddy bear
- ☐ TV set
- ☐ Voodoo doll
- ☐ Yo-yo

Suddenly...

...Frankie is lost in the outside world! There are so many sights and sounds, and so much to see. Maybe he can find a new meeting place for the monsters.

FIND FRANKIE ON THE STREET AND...

☐ Alien
☐ Bird singing
☐ Bowling ball
☐ Cat
☐ Elephant
☐ Falling flowerpot
☐ Fire hydrants (3)
☐ Flower van
☐ Football
☐ Guitar
☐ Hamburger
☐ Humpty Dumpty
☐ Karate bird
☐ King
☐ Kite
☐ Monkey
☐ Moose
☐ Mummy
☐ Ostrich
☐ Pizza
☐ Pogo stick
☐ Quicksand
☐ Rocket
☐ Santa Claus
☐ Scarecrow
☐ Tennis player
☐ Toothbrush
☐ Tuba
☐ Turtle
☐ Viking
☐ Water-skier

Frankie wonders where he should go first.

Wow! There's a lot going on in this store! Frankie can easily get lost in this dizzy, busy place.

FIND FRANKIE IN THE SUPER SUPERMARKET AND...

- ☐ Banana peel
- ☐ Basketball
- ☐ Bird
- ☐ Boat
- ☐ Bone
- ☐ Cactus
- ☐ Candles (2)
- ☐ Carrots
- ☐ Cheerleader
- ☐ Clown
- ☐ Duck
- ☐ Elephant
- ☐ "Fido"
- ☐ Fish heads
- ☐ Hammock
- ☐ Igloo
- ☐ Jack-o'-lantern
- ☐ Marshmallow
- ☐ Mermaid
- ☐ Mouse
- ☐ Periscope
- ☐ Ping-Pong ball
- ☐ Roller skates
- ☐ Six other monsters
- ☐ Skull
- ☐ Snowman
- ☐ Surfer
- ☐ Thief
- ☐ Tin Man
- ☐ Toast
- ☐ Wagon
- ☐ Witch
- ☐ Yo-yo

After all this activity, Frankie needs to find a quiet, dark place to relax.

Unfortunately, this show is so bad that even a nice monster like Frankie can't watch it for long.

FIND FRANKIE AT THE THEATER AND...

- ☐ Alligator
- ☐ Arrows (2)
- ☐ Camel
- ☐ Candle
- ☐ Chicken
- ☐ Clipboard
- ☐ Cowboy
- ☐ Deer
- ☐ Elephants (3)
- ☐ Fire hydrant
- ☐ Fish (4)
- ☐ Frog
- ☐ Ghosts (3)
- ☐ Giraffe
- ☐ Hammer
- ☐ Jack-in-the-box
- ☐ Jack-o'-lantern
- ☐ Lost shoe
- ☐ Mice (3)
- ☐ Octopus
- ☐ Paintbrush
- ☐ Peter Pan
- ☐ Pillow
- ☐ Satellite dish
- ☐ Snail
- ☐ Star
- ☐ Tin Man
- ☐ TV set
- ☐ Umbrellas (2)

Frankie needs some fresh air. So it's off to...

...a place where the creatures look even stranger than he does. Some have fur and some have feathers. Some have horns. Some are scary!

FIND FRANKIE AT THE ZOO AND...

- ☐ Baby taking a bath
- ☐ Balloons (6)
- ☐ Beach balls (3)
- ☐ Books (2)
- ☐ Brooms (2)
- ☐ Cactus
- ☐ Camera
- ☐ Cowboy
- ☐ Dunce cap
- ☐ Elf
- ☐ Fisherman
- ☐ Flamingo
- ☐ Ghosts (2)
- ☐ Heart
- ☐ Ice-cream cones (2)
- ☐ Kite
- ☐ Old tire
- ☐ Picnic basket
- ☐ Quarter moon
- ☐ Robin Hood
- ☐ Sailor
- ☐ Santa Claus
- ☐ Skateboard
- ☐ Socks (2)
- ☐ Stepladder
- ☐ Telescope
- ☐ Tick-tack-toe
- ☐ Trash baskets (3)
- ☐ Turtle
- ☐ Witch

After the zoo, Frankie is a little hungry...

...so he goes to look for something to eat. He wonders if they serve his favorite monster mash here. Perhaps this would be a good place for the monsters to meet.

Before he gets lost again...

FIND FRANKIE AT THE YUM-YUM EMPORIUM AND...

- ☐ Arrow
- ☐ Birdcage
- ☐ Bone
- ☐ Chicken man
- ☐ Cook
- ☐ Dogs (3)
- ☐ Fishing pole
- ☐ Football
- ☐ Knight
- ☐ Mailbox
- ☐ Manager
- ☐ Panda
- ☐ Pirate
- ☐ Princess
- ☐ Robot
- ☐ Rubber duck
- ☐ Salt shaker
- ☐ Scuba diver
- ☐ Sheriff
- ☐ Skulls (2)
- ☐ Space creature
- ☐ Star
- ☐ Straws (2)
- ☐ Sunglasses (2)
- ☐ Tombstone
- ☐ Tray of pizza
- ☐ Tuba
- ☐ Turtles (2)
- ☐ Volcano
- ☐ Wig

After lunch, Frankie wanders into the aquarium to see some underwater monsters. Even though they're all wet, they seem to be having a good time.

FIND FRANKIE IN THE AQUARIUM AND...

- ☐ Boat
- ☐ Bucket
- ☐ Cans of tuna
- ☐ Cat
- ☐ Diver
- ☐ Dog
- ☐ Duck
- ☐ Ear
- ☐ Eyeglasses
- ☐ Fisherman
- ☐ Flying fish
- ☐ Guitar
- ☐ Hammer
- ☐ Hearts (4)
- ☐ Ice skater
- ☐ Igloo
- ☐ Life preserver
- ☐ Mermaid
- ☐ Magnifying glass
- ☐ Merman
- ☐ Old-fashioned radio
- ☐ Sea horse
- ☐ Socks (2)
- ☐ Starfish (3)
- ☐ Stingray
- ☐ Submarine
- ☐ Surfer
- ☐ Swordfish (2)
- ☐ Tick-tack-toe
- ☐ Tiger
- ☐ Water leak
- ☐ Wooden leg

After watching the fish frolic, Frankie feels like having some fun too.

Hot dog! It's Frankie's first time on wheels! If only his monster friends could see him now.

FIND FRANKIE AT THE ROWDY ROLLER RINK AND...

☐ Apple
☐ Artist
☐ Basketball
☐ Bowling ball
☐ Boxer
☐ Boy Scout
☐ Cave man
☐ Centaur
☐ Centipede
☐ Convict
☐ Drum
☐ Fire hydrant
☐ Fish
☐ Ghost
☐ Giant roller skate
☐ Guitar
☐ Half-stop sign
☐ Hockey player
☐ Ice skater
☐ Jugglers (2)
☐ Paintbrushes (2)
☐ Piano
☐ Pillow
☐ Scarfs (2)
☐ Skier
☐ Snow woman
☐ Super hero
☐ Swan
☐ Three-legged skater
☐ Unicorn
☐ Weight lifter
☐ Witch
☐ Zebra

After rocking and rolling around the rink, Frankie sees a place with lots of space monsters on video screens. He hears bloops and bleeps, bzaps and bliks—sounds that Frankie's friends usually make.

FIND FRANKIE IN THE ARCADE AND...

☐ Angel
☐ Baseball
☐ Bat
☐ Bathtub
☐ Bomb
☐ Bottle
☐ Bow
☐ Carrot
☐ Darts (4)
☐ Dog
☐ Earmuffs
☐ Giraffe
☐ Hammer
☐ Headless player
☐ Heart
☐ Highest score
☐ Horseshoe
☐ Ice-cream cone
☐ Jack-o'-lantern
☐ Painter
☐ Paper airplane
☐ Pillow
☐ Pinocchio
☐ Rabbit
☐ Robot
☐ Snakes (5)
☐ Spinning top
☐ Surfer
☐ Traffic ticket
☐ Trash can
☐ Wrecking ball

All the noise makes Frankie want to look for a peaceful place...

...outside of the city. This seems like a great place to live. If only he can find a nice, ugly home where the monsters can meet.

FIND FRANKIE IN THE SUBURBS AND...

- ☐ Badminton game
- ☐ Bird
- ☐ Caddy
- ☐ Candle
- ☐ Clown
- ☐ Cow
- ☐ Dogs (3)
- ☐ Duck
- ☐ Fencing star
- ☐ Fire hydrants (4)
- ☐ Flat tire
- ☐ Footballs (2)
- ☐ Hearts (3)
- ☐ Hose
- ☐ Hot dog mobile
- ☐ Ice-cream cone
- ☐ Ice skate
- ☐ Kite
- ☐ Lion
- ☐ Marching band
- ☐ Paper delivery
- ☐ Photographer
- ☐ Pig
- ☐ Pyramid
- ☐ Shark
- ☐ Telescope
- ☐ Treasure chest
- ☐ Tepee
- ☐ Umbrella
- ☐ Unicorn
- ☐ Unicycle
- ☐ Zebra

Wait! Maybe there is a place! Can you see it?

There, at the top of the hill, Frankie finds the perfect meeting house. The monsters finally find Frankie and elect him President of the Monster Club. What a great time for a party!

FIND FRANKIE AT THE MONSTERS' NEW CLUBHOUSE AND...

☐ Bats (4)
☐ Bones (4)
☐ Bottle
☐ Candles (2)
☐ Clock
☐ Coffeepot
☐ Coffin
☐ Cup
☐ Dog
☐ Flower
☐ Flying carpet
☐ Football
☐ Ghosts (5)
☐ Happy star
☐ Headless man
☐ Light bulb
☐ Mail carrier
☐ Mouse
☐ Mummy
☐ Octopus
☐ Pencil sharpener
☐ Skulls (4)
☐ Sled
☐ Snake
☐ Sword
☐ Tick-tack-toe
☐ Tombstones (2)
☐ Thirteens (4)
☐ Three-headed monster
☐ Top hat
☐ TV set
☐ Two-headed monster
☐ Umbrella
☐ Witch

FIND FRANKIE   SEARCH FOR SUSIE   LOOK FOR LAURA   DETECT DONALD

LOOK FOR LAURA

Laura lives on a planet called MAXX. One day she decided to visit her grandmother in her astro-ferry. All her friends came to say good-bye.

LOOK FOR LAURA ON THE PLANET MAXX AND...

☐ Balloons (3)
☐ Birdhouse
☐ Birds (2)
☐ Books (3)
☐ Clipboard
☐ Clocks (4)
☐ Coffeepot
☐ Covered wagon
☐ Dog
☐ Elephant
☐ Evergreen tree
☐ Fish
☐ Flowerpot
☐ Footballs (2)
☐ Fork
☐ Graduate
☐ Hamburger
☐ Hot dog
☐ Ice-cream pop
☐ Jump rope
☐ Kite
☐ Old radio
☐ Old tire
☐ Pizza
☐ Sled
☐ Tepee
☐ Train engine
☐ Turtle
☐ TV set
☐ Umbrella

But when Laura got into the astro-ferry, she pressed the wrong button.

Suddenly she was in an alien world surrounded by strange-looking creatures. Everything was wet! This wasn't her grandmother's house. This wasn't MAXX. This wasn't even land!

LOOK FOR LAURA IN THE OCEAN AND...

☐ Anchovy
☐ Bats (2)
☐ Bell
☐ Books (2)
☐ Bow
☐ Cheese
☐ Crown
☐ Cup
☐ Fire hydrant
☐ Flowers (2)
☐ Ghost
☐ Guitar
☐ Hammer
☐ Haystack
☐ Heart
☐ Horseshoe
☐ Ice-cream cone
☐ Key
☐ Mermaid
☐ Needlefish
☐ Octopus
☐ Old tire
☐ Pencil
☐ Pizza
☐ Saw
☐ Seesaw
☐ Snail
☐ Straw hat
☐ Telescope
☐ Treasure chest
☐ Turtles (3)
☐ TV set
☐ Umbrella

Laura zoomed up and finally landed...

...in a jungle watering hole. There the creatures were furry and feathery.

LOOK FOR LAURA AT THE WATERING HOLE AND...

☐ Arrow
☐ Balloons (3)
☐ Beach ball
☐ Birdbath
☐ Bird's nest
☐ Boat
☐ Bones (3)
☐ Camel
☐ Camera
☐ Crocodile
☐ Donkey
☐ Feather
☐ Football
☐ Giraffe
☐ Heart
☐ Jack-o'-lantern
☐ Joe of the jungle
☐ Lion
☐ Lollipop
☐ Owl
☐ Pelican
☐ Periscope
☐ Pig
☐ Rooster
☐ Snake
☐ Socks (2)
☐ Tin can
☐ Toucan
☐ Unicorn
☐ Wart hog
☐ Wolf
☐ Worm
☐ Yo-yo

But Laura wasn't sure if they were all friendly, so she got back on board and decided to explore the rest of this strange world.

As Laura flew through the sky, she saw some mountains covered with white stuff. Laura landed and for the very first time she saw— SNOW! This was fun! She wished her friends on MAXX could see the snow too.

LOOK FOR LAURA ON A SKI SLOPE IN THE ALPS AND...

- ☐ Alligator
- ☐ Artist
- ☐ Automobile
- ☐ Boat
- ☐ Bone
- ☐ Bunny
- ☐ Camel
- ☐ Cold telephone
- ☐ Dog
- ☐ Elf
- ☐ Evergreen tree
- ☐ Fish
- ☐ Football player
- ☐ Hammock
- ☐ Igloo
- ☐ Jack-o'-lantern
- ☐ Kite
- ☐ Mailbox
- ☐ Mouse
- ☐ Rake
- ☐ Santa Claus
- ☐ Scuba diver
- ☐ Skateboard
- ☐ Sleeping monster
- ☐ Snowman
- ☐ Sunglasses
- ☐ Top hat
- ☐ Turtle
- ☐ TV antenna
- ☐ Uphill skier

Then she was frightened by a loud yodel and away she went.

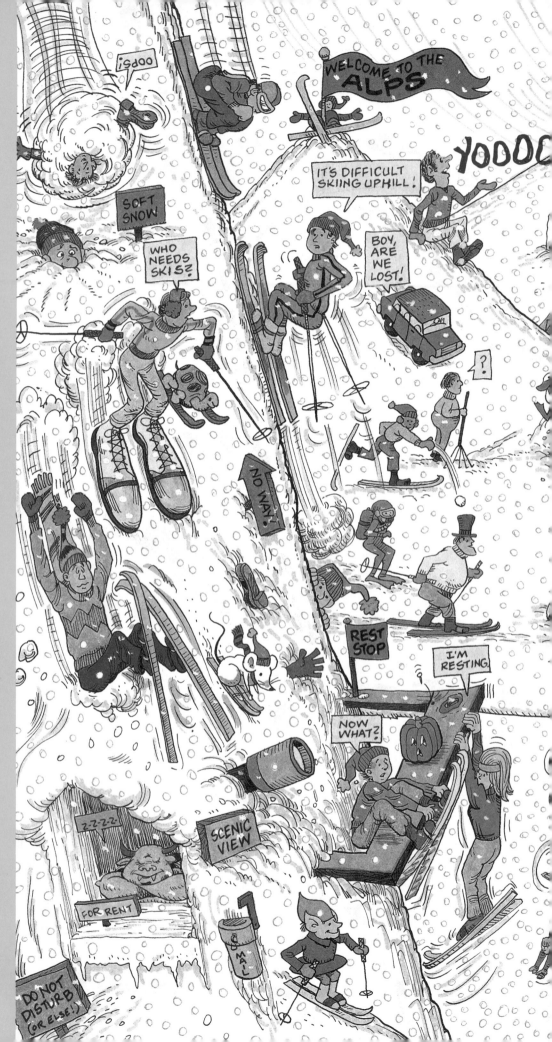

Laura flew south and landed in the desert—or rather, an oasis in the desert. Wow, it was hot! And people had towels on their heads! Everyone was too busy buying and selling at the bazaar to notice Laura, so she continued on her journey.

LOOK FOR LAURA AT THE BAH-HA BAZAAR AND...

☐ Beach ball
☐ Bird
☐ Broom
☐ Cat
☐ Clouds (2)
☐ Coconuts (4)
☐ Dog
☐ Donkey
☐ Elephant
☐ Flying carpets (2)
☐ Football
☐ Genie
☐ Horn
☐ Ice-cream cone
☐ Igloo
☐ Kite
☐ Necklace
☐ Oil well
☐ Pillow fight
☐ Rabbit
☐ Shovel
☐ Skier
☐ Sled
☐ Snail
☐ Snakes (4)
☐ Straw baskets (2)
☐ Sunglasses
☐ Telescope
☐ Tents (4)
☐ Truck
☐ Turtle
☐ Umbrella

Back north went the astro-ferry. Laura saw many beautiful places as she flew over Europe, so she decided to visit them.

LOOK FOR LAURA IN EUROPE AND...

☐ Automobiles (2)
☐ Ball
☐ Ballerinas (2)
☐ Boats (3)
☐ Cancan dancers
☐ Castle
☐ Dog
☐ Donkey
☐ Egret
☐ Fisherman
☐ Flying fish
☐ Ghost
☐ Gondola
☐ Hot-air balloon
☐ King
☐ Knight in armor
☐ Non-flying fish (3)
☐ Periscope
☐ Reindeer
☐ Skier
☐ Snake
☐ Snowmen (2)
☐ Starfish
☐ Stork
☐ Telescope
☐ Tour bus
☐ Train
☐ Tulips
☐ Turtle
☐ Windmill

Laura was beginning to get homesick and she wondered how she would find her way back to MAXX.

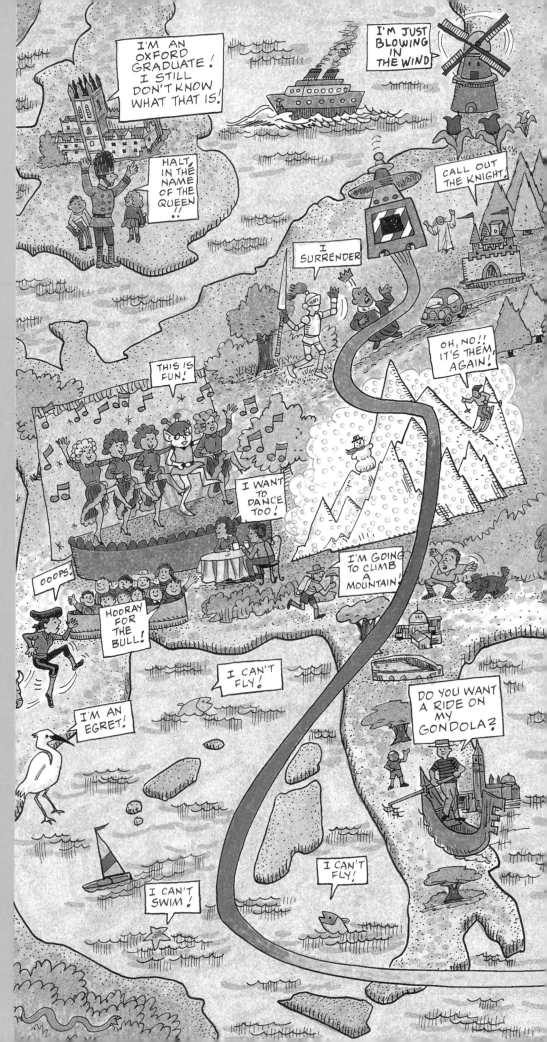

From the astro-ferry, Laura spotted a large group of children doing different activities. Maybe they could help.

LOOK FOR LAURA AT SUMMER CAMP AND...

- ☐ Alligator
- ☐ Basket
- ☐ Bats (2)
- ☐ Bear
- ☐ Broom
- ☐ Candy cane
- ☐ Cannon
- ☐ Cheese
- ☐ Cooks (2)
- ☐ Duck
- ☐ Firefighter
- ☐ Fish
- ☐ Head of a monster
- ☐ Headless monster
- ☐ Jack-o'-lantern
- ☐ Lake
- ☐ Lamp
- ☐ Motorcycle
- ☐ Owl
- ☐ Paper airplane
- ☐ Pizza
- ☐ Scarecrow
- ☐ Shovel
- ☐ Skateboard
- ☐ Skulls (2)
- ☐ Stepladder
- ☐ Target
- ☐ Telephone
- ☐ Three-legged chair
- ☐ Tin can
- ☐ Toy duck
- ☐ Wagon
- ☐ Witch

Laura had never seen so many strange activities. And no one had ever heard of the planet, MAXX.

The kids at camp directed Laura to a huge tent down the road. In the center of the tent, silly people, and animals too, seemed to be having fun.

LOOK FOR LAURA AT THE CIRCUS AND...

☐ Bad juggler
☐ Banana peel
☐ Binoculars
☐ Bowling ball
☐ Bow tie
☐ Cactus
☐ Cheese
☐ Cowboy hats (2)
☐ Dry paint
☐ Elephants (2)
☐ Ghost
☐ Hot dog
☐ Ice-cream cone
☐ Knight in armor
☐ Lion
☐ Lost shoe
☐ Monkey suit
☐ Mouse
☐ Picture frame
☐ Pie
☐ Pig
☐ Pirate
☐ Shoe shine box
☐ Skateboards (3)
☐ Top hat
☐ Training wheels
☐ Umbrella
☐ Walking flower
☐ Watering can

Laura enjoyed herself at the circus, but she was worried about getting home.

She tried again to get the astro-ferry to head for MAXX. Instead, she landed in a noisy city. Laura was about to give up hope of ever returning home. Then she saw some beings that looked a little like herself.

LOOK FOR LAURA IN WASHINGTON D.C. AND...

- ☐ Artist
- ☐ Birds (2)
- ☐ Bones (3)
- ☐ Books (3)
- ☐ Bows (4)
- ☐ Brush
- ☐ Camera
- ☐ Campaign poster
- ☐ Cat
- ☐ Envelope
- ☐ Goose
- ☐ Hammer
- ☐ Hard hats (2)
- ☐ Hot-air balloon
- ☐ Jogger
- ☐ Kangaroo
- ☐ Kite
- ☐ Magnifying glass
- ☐ Pentagon
- ☐ "People Working"
- ☐ Sailor's hat
- ☐ Scarecrow
- ☐ Secret agent
- ☐ Sleeping man
- ☐ Toolbox
- ☐ Turtle
- ☐ Tyrannosaurus
- ☐ Wagon
- ☐ Washington Monument

Perhaps they could help her, so she followed them as they walked...

...back to school! In the classroom, Laura watched the children do their spelling lessons. H-O-M-E spelled home.

LOOK FOR LAURA AT SCHOOL AND...

- ☐ Alexander
- ☐ Bat
- ☐ Bells (2)
- ☐ Broom
- ☐ Bubble gum
- ☐ Cat
- ☐ Clothespin
- ☐ Cupcake
- ☐ Drummer
- ☐ Easel
- ☐ Fish (2)
- ☐ Footballs (2)
- ☐ Globe
- ☐ Golf club
- ☐ Half moon
- ☐ Happy face
- ☐ Hats (2)
- ☐ Heart
- ☐ Hourglass
- ☐ Igloo
- ☐ Jump rope
- ☐ Monster mask
- ☐ Owl
- ☐ Paintbrush
- ☐ Pinocchio
- ☐ Plate
- ☐ Protoceratops
- ☐ Robin
- ☐ Robot
- ☐ School bags (2)
- ☐ Scissors
- ☐ Snow
- ☐ Soccer ball
- ☐ Stocking
- ☐ Sunglasses
- ☐ Wastepaper basket

Suddenly, Laura decided to type "M-A-X-X" in the astro-ferry's computer.

It worked! The astro-ferry zoomed home! Everyone was gathered to welcome her back to MAXX. Laura told them all about the many strange and wonderful things she had seen on Earth.

LOOK FOR LAURA AT THE WELCOME HOME PARTY AND...

☐ Alien-in-the-box
☐ Baseball cap
☐ Basket
☐ Bone
☐ Candle
☐ Carrot
☐ Cheese
☐ Cupcake
☐ Evergreen tree
☐ Falling stars (7)
☐ Fire hydrant
☐ Football
☐ Graduate
☐ Guitar
☐ Hamburger
☐ Hammer
☐ Hot dog
☐ Ice-cream soda
☐ Light bulb
☐ Meatball
☐ Mouse
☐ Pencils (2)
☐ Rose
☐ Screwdriver
☐ Shovel
☐ Snail
☐ Tent
☐ Turtle
☐ TV set
☐ Unicorn
☐ Yo-yo

From now on, Laura will be very careful when she travels in her astro-ferry.

DETECT DONALD   FIND FRANKIE   SEARCH FOR SUSIE   LOOK FOR LAURA

SEARCH FOR SUSIE

One day Susie's mom and dad took her to the Big Fun Amusement Park. Susie was excited and couldn't wait to see all the rides. While her parents were buying popcorn, Susie wandered off and started to explore the park.

SEARCH FOR SUSIE IN THE BIG FUN PARK AND...

- ☐ Banana peel
- ☐ Bowling ball
- ☐ Burst balloon
- ☐ Camel
- ☐ Candle
- ☐ Clothesline
- ☐ Clown-o-saurus (3)
- ☐ Ducks (2)
- ☐ Ear of corn
- ☐ Egg
- ☐ Football
- ☐ Ghost
- ☐ Hearts (2)
- ☐ Ice-cream cone
- ☐ Jack-o'-lantern
- ☐ Juggler
- ☐ Magnifying glass
- ☐ Megaphone
- ☐ Octopus
- ☐ Pencil
- ☐ Periscopes (2)
- ☐ Police (6)
- ☐ Raccoon
- ☐ Red wagon
- ☐ Reindeer
- ☐ Socks (2)
- ☐ Sour-puss-saurus
- ☐ Turtle
- ☐ Violinist

"Where's Susie?" asked her father.

"I don't know," answered her mother. "But we'd better start looking for her."

Meanwhile, Susie heard lots of shouting and splashing. Everyone seemed to be having fun. Or were they?

SEARCH FOR SUSIE AT THE WATER RIDE AND...

- ☐ Bone
- ☐ Bride
- ☐ Cactus
- ☐ Candy canes (2)
- ☐ Cupcake
- ☐ Curtains
- ☐ Dogs (2)
- ☐ Egg
- ☐ Fire hydrant
- ☐ Fish (4)
- ☐ Flying horse
- ☐ Goat
- ☐ Ground hog
- ☐ Hearts (3)
- ☐ Hobbyhorse
- ☐ Hot dog
- ☐ Island
- ☐ Moby Dick
- ☐ Nightmare
- ☐ Peter Pan
- ☐ Pickle barrel
- ☐ Police-o-saurus
- ☐ Sailboat
- ☐ Sea horse
- ☐ Surfboard
- ☐ Tuba
- ☐ Umbrella

Susie left the Water Ride and headed for the carousel. Around and around it went. Susie thought she heard her parents calling her, but with all the noise and excitement she couldn't find them.

SEARCH FOR SUSIE AT THE CAROUSEL AND...

- ☐ Alarm clock
- ☐ Ball
- ☐ Bat
- ☐ Broom
- ☐ Butterfly
- ☐ Cannon
- ☐ Dancing bears (2)
- ☐ Dentist
- ☐ Ear
- ☐ Fan
- ☐ Frog
- ☐ Golf bag
- ☐ Kangaroo
- ☐ Lamp
- ☐ Lollipop
- ☐ Mushroom
- ☐ Neckties (3)
- ☐ Parrot
- ☐ Pig
- ☐ Roller skate
- ☐ Scarecrow
- ☐ Snake
- ☐ Snow lady
- ☐ Super hero
- ☐ Telescope
- ☐ Top hat
- ☐ Truck
- ☐ Turtles (2)
- ☐ Unicorn
- ☐ Yo-yo

Susie's next stop was the Fun House. Wow! Things were really wild in there! Susie's mom and dad were searching for her in the Fun House too.

SEARCH FOR SUSIE IN THE FUN HOUSE AND...

- ☐ Banana peel
- ☐ Barrel
- ☐ Bib
- ☐ Cave man
- ☐ Cup
- ☐ Football helmet
- ☐ Headless body
- ☐ Humpty Dumpty
- ☐ Igloo
- ☐ Jack-in-a-box
- ☐ Jack-o'-lantern
- ☐ Kite
- ☐ Magician
- ☐ Medal
- ☐ Parachute
- ☐ Pie
- ☐ Pillow
- ☐ Pot
- ☐ Puppy
- ☐ Saw
- ☐ Sled
- ☐ Snake
- ☐ Sock
- ☐ Stool
- ☐ Susie's parents
- ☐ Target
- ☐ Traffic light
- ☐ Train engine
- ☐ Wacky clock
- ☐ Watermelon slice
- ☐ Wreath

Susie finally found her way through the maze and out of the Fun House. Then she heard loud, squeaking sounds which she followed to a huge, spinning Ferris wheel. "What a neat park this is," thought Susie.

SEARCH FOR SUSIE AT THE FERRIS WHEEL AND...

- ☐ Arrow
- ☐ Astronaut
- ☐ Birdhouse
- ☐ Broom
- ☐ Camera
- ☐ Candy cane
- ☐ Chimney
- ☐ Copycat
- ☐ Dinosaur guitarist
- ☐ Eye
- ☐ Golfer
- ☐ Hammock
- ☐ Hockey stick
- ☐ Ice skates
- ☐ Kite
- ☐ Lions (2)
- ☐ Oil can
- ☐ "Oup and Doup"
- ☐ Painters (2)
- ☐ Papa bear
- ☐ Plumber's plunger
- ☐ Santa Claus
- ☐ Screw
- ☐ Star
- ☐ Surfer
- ☐ Susie's parents
- ☐ Telephone
- ☐ Ticket collector
- ☐ Umbrella
- ☐ Watering can

Susie couldn't resist a ride on a roller coaster. Even an old, rickety-looking roller coaster. She bought a ticket and off she went!

SEARCH FOR SUSIE ON THE ROCK AND ROLLER COASTER RIDE AND...

☐ Balloons (5)
☐ Bat
☐ Birdcage
☐ Boat
☐ Can
☐ Carrot
☐ Cave man
☐ Dino-in-a-bottle
☐ Drummer
☐ Firefighter
☐ Fire hydrant
☐ Flames
☐ Flower eater
☐ Mailbox
☐ Moose
☐ Mummy
☐ Police-o-saurus
☐ Rabbits (5)
☐ Red tire
☐ Rocket
☐ Safe
☐ Skateboard
☐ Skier
☐ Sock
☐ Tennis racket
☐ Tick-tack-toe
☐ Unicycle
☐ Weights
☐ Window
☐ Wreath

Meanwhile, Susie's parents were still searching for her.

After a thrilling ride on the roller coaster, Susie needed a nice, quiet place to relax. The Game Room seemed like the perfect spot. Not much was happening there.

SEARCH FOR SUSIE IN THE GAME ROOM AND...

☐ Apples (2)
☐ Baseball
☐ Basketball
☐ Bomb
☐ Boomerang
☐ Can
☐ Candle
☐ Carrot
☐ Coffeepot
☐ Cup
☐ Dice
☐ Donkey's tail
☐ Dracula
☐ Earmuffs
☐ Ghost
☐ Gift box
☐ Graduate
☐ Guitar
☐ Hammer
☐ Horseshoe
☐ Pencil
☐ Poodle
☐ Sailboat
☐ Telescope
☐ Timekeeper
☐ Top hat
☐ Turtles (3)
☐ Umpire
☐ Unicorn
☐ Yo-yo

Susie played a few games, then headed for...

...the bumper cars! What an exciting ride that was! Susie banged and bumped and crashed her way from one end to the other. She waved to her parents who unfortunately got bumped before they could see her.

SEARCH FOR SUSIE ON THE BUMPER CARS AND...

- ☐ Alien
- ☐ Artist
- ☐ Banana peel
- ☐ Birdcage
- ☐ Bride
- ☐ Cactus
- ☐ Camel
- ☐ Candy cane
- ☐ Cans (5)
- ☐ Car "007"
- ☐ Car "8A"
- ☐ Car "54"
- ☐ Cat
- ☐ Crown
- ☐ Fire hydrant
- ☐ Giraffes (2)
- ☐ Hot dog
- ☐ Ice-cream cone
- ☐ Jack-o'-lantern
- ☐ Kite
- ☐ Light bulb
- ☐ Mice (2)
- ☐ Musician
- ☐ Pig
- ☐ Police (2)
- ☐ Shoemobile
- ☐ Speed limit
- ☐ Stars (2)
- ☐ Sunglasses
- ☐ Surfer
- ☐ Target

After a long day of fun, Susie was getting hungry. She wondered where she might find a delicious banana split. Then Susie spotted a giant ice-cream cone.

SEARCH FOR SUSIE AT THE ICE-CREAM SHOP AND...

- ☐ Bad-news lizard
- ☐ Balloons (3)
- ☐ Clock
- ☐ Drum
- ☐ Eyeglasses
- ☐ Fish
- ☐ Fudge pop
- ☐ Igloo
- ☐ Kangaroo
- ☐ King Kong
- ☐ Mushroom
- ☐ Paint bucket
- ☐ Santa Claus
- ☐ Sled
- ☐ Slice of pie
- ☐ Snail
- ☐ Socks (2)
- ☐ Sombrero
- ☐ Spoon
- ☐ Teeth
- ☐ Telescope
- ☐ Tepee
- ☐ Tire
- ☐ Top hat
- ☐ Toy duck
- ☐ Toy train
- ☐ TV set
- ☐ Umbrella
- ☐ Unicorn

Mom and Dad were still searching and searching for Susie. And...

...there she was! On the giant swings! Susie couldn't wait to tell them about all the fun she had in the Big Fun Amusement Park.

SEARCH FOR SUSIE ON THE GIANT SWINGS AND...

- ☐ Bat
- ☐ Bell
- ☐ Birdhouse
- ☐ Blue sneaker
- ☐ Bone
- ☐ Broken ropes (3)
- ☐ Broom
- ☐ Bucket of red paint
- ☐ Candle
- ☐ Car
- ☐ Carrot
- ☐ Chickens (2)
- ☐ Fish
- ☐ Football
- ☐ Fork
- ☐ Genie
- ☐ Horn
- ☐ Human acrobats (2)
- ☐ Ice-cream cone
- ☐ Ice skate
- ☐ Magnifying glass
- ☐ Paper airplane
- ☐ Parachute
- ☐ Scissors
- ☐ Slingshot
- ☐ Snake
- ☐ Soccer ball
- ☐ Stars (4)
- ☐ Ticket collector
- ☐ Top hat
- ☐ Waiter
- ☐ Wrecking ball

SEARCH FOR SUSIE   LOOK FOR LAURA   DETECT DONALD   FIND FRANKIE

WHERE ARE THEY?

Travel the world to find Freddie.

Travel through time to look for Lisa.

Search high and low for Sylvester.

Find out where Wendy could possibly be!

FIND FREDDIE: AROUND THE WORLD

LOOK FOR LISA: TIME TRAVELER

SEARCH FOR SYLVESTER

WHERE'S WENDY?

FREDDIE

LISA

WENDY

SYLVESTER

FIND FREDDIE AROUND THE WORLD

Freddie has won an around the world vacation…and you're invited to come along! Stay close to Freddie, or you might get lost!

FIND FREDDIE IN THE UNITED STATES AND…

- ☐ Balloons (2)
- ☐ Barn
- ☐ Brooms (2)
- ☐ Buffalo
- ☐ Cactus (4)
- ☐ Campfire
- ☐ Cannon
- ☐ Cows (2)
- ☐ Coyote
- ☐ Footballs (2)
- ☐ Ghost
- ☐ Goat
- ☐ Guitars (2)
- ☐ Hockey player
- ☐ Jack-o´-lantern
- ☐ Kite
- ☐ Lighthouse
- ☐ Log cabin
- ☐ Moose
- ☐ Owl
- ☐ Periscope
- ☐ Scarecrows (2)
- ☐ Star
- ☐ Statue of Liberty
- ☐ Surfer
- ☐ Turtle
- ☐ Witch

Where did the elephant escape from?
Who is sleeping?
Where is Cuba?
What's on sale?
Where's the big cheese?

Freddie is northward bound as he travels to Canada, Alaska, Greenland, and Iceland.

FIND FREDDIE IN THIS WINTER WONDERLAND AND...

- ☐ Automobile
- ☐ Banana peel
- ☐ Bear
- ☐ Beaver
- ☐ Birds (2)
- ☐ Bone
- ☐ Box
- ☐ Bucket
- ☐ Elephant
- ☐ Elf
- ☐ Horse
- ☐ Ice-cream cone
- ☐ Igloo
- ☐ Jackrabbit
- ☐ Jester
- ☐ King Kong
- ☐ Lumberjack
- ☐ Mounty
- ☐ Oil well
- ☐ Pencil
- ☐ Pumpkin
- ☐ Scarecrow
- ☐ Seal
- ☐ Sleds (2)
- ☐ Snow castle
- ☐ Snowmen (2)
- ☐ Stars (2)
- ☐ Top hat
- ☐ Totem pole
- ☐ Unicycles

Where did Freddie take French lessons?
What's the 49th state?
Where's Greenland?
What's the capital of Canada?
Where's Nova Scotia?

Freddie heads southeast to the next three stops on his world tour: Ireland, Scotland, and England.

FIND FREDDIE IN THE BRITISH ISLES AND...

- ☐ Airplane
- ☐ Bagpiper
- ☐ Boats (7)
- ☐ Book
- ☐ Broom
- ☐ Bus
- ☐ Chicken
- ☐ Crown
- ☐ Dog
- ☐ Fish (8)
- ☐ Four-leaf clovers (4)
- ☐ Guitar
- ☐ Harp
- ☐ Horseshoe
- ☐ Kite
- ☐ Knight
- ☐ Magnifying glass
- ☐ Periscope
- ☐ Pig
- ☐ Pot of gold
- ☐ Sheep (3)
- ☐ Spear
- ☐ Stonehenge
- ☐ Telescope
- ☐ Turtle
- ☐ Umbrella

What games are they playing? (4)
What's for sale? (2)
Where's France?
Who did Freddie visit in Ireland?

Freddie travels on throughout Europe...and you go along with him!

FIND FREDDIE AMONG THESE FRIENDLY FOREIGNERS AND...

- ☐ Artist
- ☐ Bather
- ☐ Beachball
- ☐ Bone
- ☐ Bull
- ☐ Camel
- ☐ Castle
- ☐ Dogs (2)
- ☐ Envelope
- ☐ Fire hydrant
- ☐ Heart
- ☐ Jack-o´-lantern
- ☐ Key
- ☐ Laundry
- ☐ Lost and Found
- ☐ Motorcycle
- ☐ Mountain goat
- ☐ Pencil
- ☐ Rabbit
- ☐ Sailboats (2)
- ☐ Santa Claus
- ☐ Skier
- ☐ Snowmen (2)
- ☐ Stars (2)
- ☐ Stork
- ☐ Tulip
- ☐ Turtles (2)
- ☐ Volcano
- ☐ Witch

Who was forgotten?
What gets wet?
Where do pandas live?
Where's the Strait of Gibraltar?

Next, Freddie is off to explore the largest continent, Asia. There are many things here that he's always wanted to see.

FIND FREDDIE IN THIS VAST AND EXOTIC LAND AND...

- ☐ Accordian player
- ☐ Balloon
- ☐ Bears (2)
- ☐ Birdcage
- ☐ Candy cane
- ☐ Chef
- ☐ Dragons (2)
- ☐ Fan
- ☐ Flying carpet
- ☐ Genie
- ☐ Heart
- ☐ Horse
- ☐ Kite
- ☐ Lemming
- ☐ Nutmeg tree
- ☐ Pandas (3)
- ☐ Peacock
- ☐ Reindeer
- ☐ Rice field
- ☐ Snakes (2)
- ☐ Surfer
- ☐ Tea cup
- ☐ Tears
- ☐ Telescope
- ☐ Tigers (2)
- ☐ Tire
- ☐ Turtle
- ☐ Water buffalo
- ☐ Yak

Where is the highest place on earth?
Which way is the North Pole?
Where's Japan?
Who needs the oasis?

Freddie's next stop is a continent filled with amazing animals. I hope he doesn't get into any trouble there.

FIND FREDDIE IN THIS AFRICAN ADVENTURE-LAND AND...

- ☐ Aardvark
- ☐ Automobile
- ☐ Book
- ☐ Boot
- ☐ Bottle
- ☐ Camels (2)
- ☐ Cape buffalo
- ☐ Cape seal
- ☐ Crocodile
- ☐ Cup
- ☐ Date palm
- ☐ Drum
- ☐ Giraffes (2)
- ☐ Gnu
- ☐ Gorilla
- ☐ Heart
- ☐ Huts (4)
- ☐ Ibis
- ☐ Leopard
- ☐ Light bulb
- ☐ Monkeys (3)
- ☐ Ostrich
- ☐ Pelican
- ☐ Penguin
- ☐ Porcupine
- ☐ Rhino
- ☐ Snakes (3)
- ☐ Sunglasses (4)
- ☐ Top hat
- ☐ TV antennas (2)
- ☐ Umbrella

Who's the king of the jungle?
Who's wearing stripes?
Where's the Suez Canal?

Freddie arrives in Australia and takes a very interesting ride. He'll stop off in New Zealand, New Guinea, and Tasmania, too.

FIND FREDDIE IN THE LAND DOWN UNDER AND...

- ☐ Barbell
- ☐ Baseball bat
- ☐ Book
- ☐ Boomerang
- ☐ Chef
- ☐ Crane
- ☐ Dingo
- ☐ Dragon
- ☐ Fishermen (2)
- ☐ Football
- ☐ Ghost
- ☐ Golfer
- ☐ Horse
- ☐ Jogger
- ☐ Kite
- ☐ Koalas (3)
- ☐ Lost shorts
- ☐ Lost sock
- ☐ Lyrebird
- ☐ Paper airplane
- ☐ Rabbits (4)
- ☐ Scuba diver
- ☐ Shark fins (5)
- ☐ Sheep (4)
- ☐ Skateboard
- ☐ Stars (3)
- ☐ Tennis players (4)
- ☐ Tent
- ☐ Tire
- ☐ Tree kangaroo
- ☐ Umbrella
- ☐ Wombat

Which three birds can't fly?
What's on sale?
Where's the Great Barrier Reef?

Freddie's next stop is the continent that surrounds the South Pole—Antarctica! It's the coldest place in the world. Is Freddie dressed for it?

FIND FREDDIE IN THIS BLISTERY BLIZZARD AND...

☐ Artist
☐ Balloon
☐ Beachball
☐ Bottle
☐ Camel
☐ Chair
☐ Chef
☐ Earmuffs
☐ Fish (2)
☐ Icebergs (4)
☐ Jester
☐ Key
☐ Lost boot
☐ Lost mitten
☐ Magnifying glass
☐ Mailbox
☐ Palm tree
☐ Penguins (10)
☐ Pick
☐ Refrigerator
☐ Seals (4)
☐ Shovel
☐ Skaters (3)
☐ Snowmen (2)
☐ South Pole
☐ Surfboard
☐ Telescope
☐ Tents (4)
☐ Tire
☐ Whales (4)

What two things are for sale?
Who's from another planet?

Watch out fourth largest continent, Freddie is coming to visit!

FIND FREDDIE IN SOUTH AMERICA AND...

- ☐ Alpaca
- ☐ Anteater
- ☐ Bear
- ☐ Binoculars
- ☐ Bone
- ☐ Bus
- ☐ Cactus
- ☐ Coffee pot
- ☐ Cowboy
- ☐ Flamingos (2)
- ☐ Flying bats (2)
- ☐ Guitar
- ☐ Hammock
- ☐ Jeep
- ☐ Monkeys (3)
- ☐ Motorcycle
- ☐ Orchid
- ☐ Periscope
- ☐ Pineapple
- ☐ Rain slicker
- ☐ Santa Claus
- ☐ Snakes (4)
- ☐ Swamp deer
- ☐ Tires (2)
- ☐ Toucans (2)
- ☐ Tree frog
- ☐ Turtles (2)
- ☐ TV antenna
- ☐ Umbrellas (2)
- ☐ Wagon

What is the longest mountain range in the world?
What's a three-sided nut?

Freddie extends his stay in South America and then heads north to Central America.

FIND FREDDIE IN BETWEEN NORTH AND SOUTH AMERICA AND…

- ☐ Aliens (2)
- ☐ Balloons (2)
- ☐ Banana boat
- ☐ Bathtub
- ☐ Bullfighter
- ☐ Butterfly
- ☐ Candle
- ☐ Flamingo
- ☐ Frog
- ☐ Iron
- ☐ Jogger
- ☐ Oil well
- ☐ Paper airplane
- ☐ Periscope
- ☐ Pirate
- ☐ Pot
- ☐ Roller skates
- ☐ Rowboat
- ☐ Sailboats (4)
- ☐ Shark fin
- ☐ Sled
- ☐ Snowman
- ☐ Straw
- ☐ Super hero
- ☐ Surfer
- ☐ Sword
- ☐ Traffic cop
- ☐ Truck
- ☐ Water-skier

Which is the largest country in Central America?
What two countries share the same island?
What's for sale? (2)
What country is separated by a canal?

It looks like some aliens have been following Freddie on his trip. Maybe they're planning to take him home with them.

FIND FREDDIE ON HIS LAST STOP AND...

- ☐ Alarm clock
- ☐ Basketball net
- ☐ Bathtub
- ☐ Bowling ball
- ☐ Castle
- ☐ Chair
- ☐ Firecracker
- ☐ Fish (8)
- ☐ Flamingo
- ☐ Giraffe
- ☐ Hot dog
- ☐ Igloo
- ☐ Jack-in-the-box
- ☐ Jack-o´-lantern
- ☐ Jackrabbit
- ☐ Kite
- ☐ Knight
- ☐ Lost ice skate
- ☐ Moose
- ☐ Owl
- ☐ Pencil
- ☐ Shark fins (2)
- ☐ Shipwrecked sailor
- ☐ Skier
- ☐ Sleds (2)
- ☐ Snowman
- ☐ Surfer
- ☐ Tepee
- ☐ Turtle
- ☐ TV antennas (3)
- ☐ Umbrella
- ☐ Walrus

Where has the walrus never been?
What country is Siberia next to?

Freddie has finally come home. All his "Where Are They?" friends are happy to see him!

FIND FREDDIE AND...

☐ Baseball cap
☐ Book
☐ Candy cane
☐ Cheese
☐ Dish
☐ Feather
☐ Fork
☐ Four-leaf clover
☐ Hearts (2)
☐ Letter
☐ Lost sock
☐ Pig
☐ Rug
☐ Slipper
☐ Star

What's for sale?
Who missed
    Freddie the most?

FIND FREDDIE
AROUND THE WORLD

Look for Lisa: Time Traveler

Lisa is going on an exciting adventure in her time-travel submarine and she wants you to come along!

LOOK FOR LISA IN PREHISTORIC TIMES AND...

- ☐ Balloons (2)
- ☐ Bathtub
- ☐ Book
- ☐ Boot
- ☐ Bottle
- ☐ Broom
- ☐ Candle
- ☐ Clown
- ☐ Coffee pot
- ☐ Cup
- ☐ Egg
- ☐ Football
- ☐ Four-leaf clover
- ☐ Hammer
- ☐ Hockey stick
- ☐ Ice-cream cone
- ☐ Ladder
- ☐ Lamp
- ☐ Necktie
- ☐ Pizza
- ☐ Ring
- ☐ Scarecrow
- ☐ Sock
- ☐ Stars (2)
- ☐ String of pearls
- ☐ Sunglasses
- ☐ Tent
- ☐ Toothbrush
- ☐ Top hat
- ☐ Umbrella
- ☐ Used tire
- ☐ Wristwatch

What hasn't been invented yet?
What's in the cup?
Is there anything for rent?

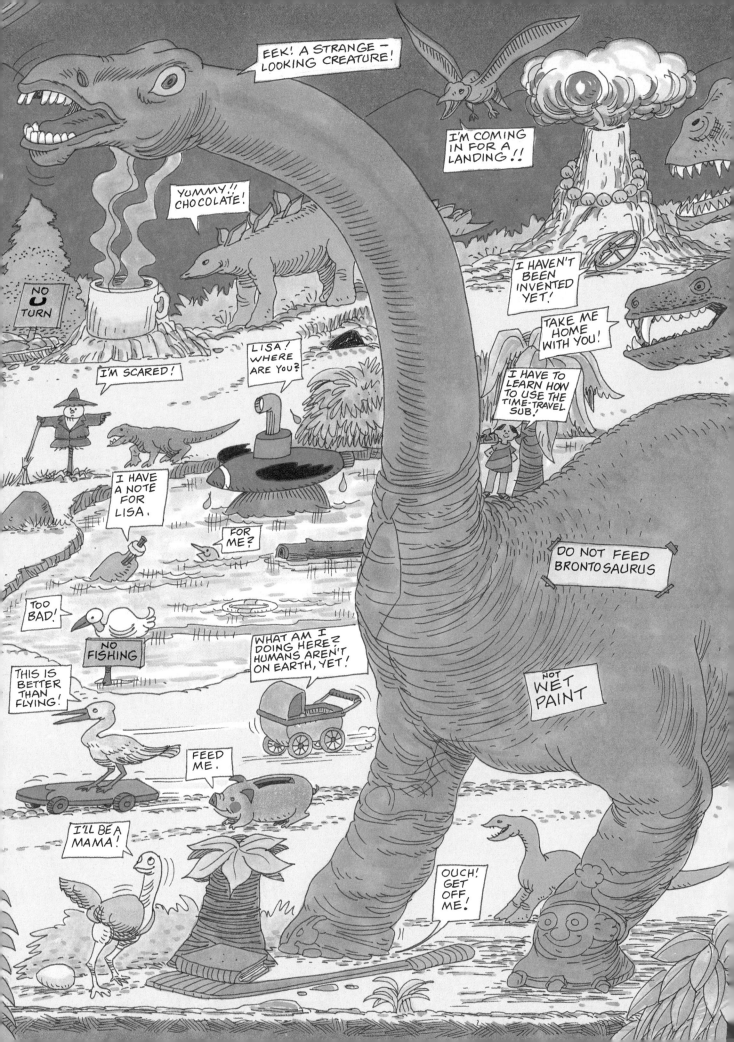

Lisa has gone forward in time and she's landed in Count Dracula's home in Transylvania.

LOOK FOR LISA IN THIS CREEPY CASTLE AND...

- ☐ Axe
- ☐ Baseball
- ☐ Bones (6)
- ☐ Books (2)
- ☐ Boomerang
- ☐ Candles (6)
- ☐ Cracked mirror
- ☐ Dart
- ☐ Dustpan
- ☐ Envelope
- ☐ Fish
- ☐ Fish skeleton
- ☐ Heart
- ☐ Keys (3)
- ☐ Mallet
- ☐ Mice (4)
- ☐ Needle
- ☐ Number 13
- ☐ Pickles
- ☐ Rabbit
- ☐ Ring
- ☐ Roller skate
- ☐ Screwdriver
- ☐ Shovel
- ☐ Skateboard
- ☐ Skulls (5)
- ☐ Spoon
- ☐ Stake
- ☐ Steak
- ☐ Sword
- ☐ Tick-tack-toe
- ☐ Top hat
- ☐ Wind-up car
- ☐ Witch's hat
- ☐ Worms (2)
- ☐ Zipper

What is
    Uncle Nutzy?
What year is it?
Where is the garlic?

Next, Lisa travels to the year 1752. She's watching Benjamin Franklin as he proves that lightning is a form of electricity.

LOOK FOR LISA AT THIS HISTORIC HAPPENING AND...

- ☐ Arrow
- ☐ Basket
- ☐ Bell
- ☐ Bifocal eyeglasses
- ☐ Brushes (2)
- ☐ Bucket
- ☐ Cane
- ☐ Corn
- ☐ Deer
- ☐ Drums (2)
- ☐ Fish
- ☐ Flowerpot
- ☐ Frog
- ☐ Ghost
- ☐ Grapes
- ☐ Hair bows (5)
- ☐ Hammer
- ☐ Hearts (2)
- ☐ Hoop
- ☐ Keys (2)
- ☐ Kites (2)
- ☐ Ladder
- ☐ Mushroom
- ☐ Pumpkin
- ☐ Rabbit
- ☐ Ring
- ☐ Snail
- ☐ Snake
- ☐ Stamp
- ☐ Stars (3)
- ☐ Surfboard
- ☐ Tepee
- ☐ Turtle
- ☐ Umbrellas (3)
- ☐ Worm

What is Mrs. Franklin's first name?
What is the name of Franklin's almanac?

Wow! The time-travel sub has landed in the middle of the Ed Sullivan show where the Beatles are performing in America for the first time.

LOOK FOR LISA AS SHE ROCKS AND ROLLS AND...

- ☐ Balloons (2)
- ☐ Banjo
- ☐ Baton
- ☐ Bird
- ☐ Book
- ☐ Bow tie
- ☐ Bubblegum bubble
- ☐ Candle
- ☐ Chef
- ☐ Count Dracula
- ☐ Cymbals
- ☐ Dog
- ☐ Earmuffs
- ☐ Envelope
- ☐ Eyeglasses (3)
- ☐ Flower
- ☐ Football
- ☐ Ghost
- ☐ Giraffe
- ☐ Hearts (2)
- ☐ Kite
- ☐ Mouse
- ☐ Party hat
- ☐ Police officer
- ☐ Propeller
- ☐ Pumpkin
- ☐ Rabbit
- ☐ Skateboard
- ☐ Snowman
- ☐ Star
- ☐ Straw hat
- ☐ Tin man
- ☐ Wagon
- ☐ Witch
- ☐ Yo-yo

How many TV cameras are there? Where were the Beatles from?

Lisa travels to Paris, France next, and arrives in the year 1902. She's in the laboratory of the first great female scientist, Madame Marie Curie.

LOOK FOR LISA AMONG THESE EXCITING EXPERIMENTS AND...

- ☐ Birds (2)
- ☐ Bone
- ☐ Book
- ☐ Broom
- ☐ Butterfly
- ☐ Cactus
- ☐ Candle
- ☐ Candy cane
- ☐ Carrot
- ☐ Clothespin
- ☐ Comb
- ☐ Compass
- ☐ Feather
- ☐ Ghost
- ☐ Hearts (2)
- ☐ Hot dog
- ☐ Ice-cream cone
- ☐ Igloo
- ☐ Keys (2)
- ☐ Mouse
- ☐ Nail
- ☐ Painted egg
- ☐ Pear
- ☐ Pencil
- ☐ Pie
- ☐ Rocket ship
- ☐ Roller skate
- ☐ Scissors
- ☐ Slice of pizza
- ☐ Straw
- ☐ Thermometer
- ☐ Toothbrush
- ☐ Tweezers

What is not dry yet?
What kind of pie is it?

Astronaut Neil Armstrong takes "a giant leap for mankind," as he thinks he's the first person to set foot on the moon. Little does he know, Lisa beat him to the moon walk!

LOOK FOR LISA IN THESE CAVERNOUS CRATERS AND...

- ☐ Airplane
- ☐ Apple
- ☐ Bat
- ☐ Book
- ☐ Bottle
- ☐ Camel
- ☐ Can
- ☐ Cat
- ☐ Chicken
- ☐ Cow
- ☐ Crown
- ☐ Dog
- ☐ Drum
- ☐ Flower
- ☐ Football
- ☐ Ghost
- ☐ Guitar
- ☐ Hammer
- ☐ Ice-cream cone
- ☐ Lips
- ☐ Mitten
- ☐ Owl
- ☐ Paintbrush
- ☐ Penguin
- ☐ Purse
- ☐ Rabbit
- ☐ Sailboat
- ☐ Seal
- ☐ Snake
- ☐ Stars (4)
- ☐ Tent
- ☐ Top hat
- ☐ Tree
- ☐ Umbrella
- ☐ Wreath

Can you find at least 12 more hidden things?

Lisa decides she wants her next trip to be a quiet sea voyage. But her time machine must have had something else in mind because Lisa has landed right in the middle of Captain Ahab's pursuit of Moby Dick!

LOOK FOR LISA IN THE OCEAN AND...

☐ Balloons (2)
☐ Beach ball
☐ Book
☐ Boomerang
☐ Bottle
☐ Candle
☐ Chef's hat
☐ Clown
☐ Drum
☐ Fire hydrant
☐ Fork
☐ Harp
☐ Harpoon
☐ Kerosene lamp
☐ Kite
☐ Lost sock
☐ Lunch box
☐ Mallet
☐ Mermaid
☐ Merman
☐ Oars (5)
☐ Pencil
☐ Picture frame
☐ Quarter moon
☐ Saw
☐ Shark fins (2)
☐ Spoon
☐ Stingray
☐ Stork
☐ Surfboard
☐ Telephone
☐ Tree
☐ Turtle
☐ Umbrella

What is the name of the whaling ship?

Lisa's time machine has traveled to a wedding party in the 1760s. Who's getting married? It's someone you may have heard of.

LOOK FOR LISA AT THIS SPECIAL CELEBRATION AND…

☐ Apple
☐ Arrow
☐ Banana
☐ Basket
☐ Boom box
☐ Broken wheel
☐ Broom
☐ Brush
☐ Elf
☐ Fiddle
☐ Fishing pole
☐ Flowerpot
☐ Fork
☐ Frog
☐ Gift
☐ Ice-cream cone
☐ Key
☐ Loaf of bread
☐ Mushroom
☐ Pear
☐ Pizza delivery
☐ Portable telephone
☐ Pumpkins (3)
☐ Rabbit
☐ Scarecrow
☐ Sherlock Holmes
☐ Skateboard
☐ Snake
☐ Soup
☐ Squirrel
☐ Top hat
☐ Wagons (2)
☐ Wedding cake
☐ Wooden spoon

What is
  Mrs. Boone's
  first name?
What's wrong
  with the table?

Lisa is now visiting the famous inventor, Thomas Edison, in his laboratory. Do you know some of the wonderful things he invented?

LOOK FOR LISA IN THE "WIZARD OF MENLO PARK'S" LAB AND...

- ☐ Ball
- ☐ Baseball cap
- ☐ Bird
- ☐ Bone
- ☐ Book
- ☐ Bucket
- ☐ Candle
- ☐ Doughnut
- ☐ Duck
- ☐ Feather
- ☐ Hard hat
- ☐ Hot dog
- ☐ Kerosene lamp
- ☐ Light bulb
- ☐ Milk container
- ☐ Mouse
- ☐ Pencils (2)
- ☐ Phonograph
- ☐ Picture frame
- ☐ Pillow
- ☐ Poodle
- ☐ Pumpkin
- ☐ Roller skates
- ☐ Safe
- ☐ Sailor's hat
- ☐ Screwdriver
- ☐ Ship
- ☐ Star
- ☐ Stool
- ☐ Sunglasses
- ☐ Typewriter
- ☐ Umbrella
- ☐ Wastepaper basket
- ☐ Wheel

What is the name of Edison's film? Who can't read?

Lisa has pushed a few too many buttons and *zap-ping-kabaa* she's landed on a distant planet in the future!

LOOK FOR LISA
AMONGST THESE
FRIENDLY ALIENS
AND…

- ☐ Apple
- ☐ Arrow
- ☐ Balloon
- ☐ Banana
- ☐ Bicycle horn
- ☐ Biplane
- ☐ Bone
- ☐ Bowling ball
- ☐ Bucket
- ☐ Captain Hook
- ☐ Clothespin
- ☐ Comb
- ☐ Cup
- ☐ Door
- ☐ Feather
- ☐ Fire hydrants (2)
- ☐ Flying saucer
- ☐ Football
- ☐ Guitar
- ☐ Heart
- ☐ Hot dog
- ☐ Ice skate
- ☐ Lock
- ☐ Nut
- ☐ Party hat
- ☐ Pie
- ☐ Sled
- ☐ Slice of pizza
- ☐ Slice of
  watermelon
- ☐ Space traffic cop
- ☐ Spoon
- ☐ Tepee
- ☐ Tire
- ☐ Watering can

What game is
  "it" late for?
What needs a target?

Lisa is trying to get back to our time zone. She's close...it's now 1925 and she's on stage at the Hippodrome Theater in New York City with the famous magician, Houdini.

LOOK FOR LISA BEFORE SHE DISAPPEARS AND...

- ☐ Balloon
- ☐ Baseball cap
- ☐ Bat
- ☐ Big apple
- ☐ Birds (2)
- ☐ Cane
- ☐ Carrot
- ☐ Chef
- ☐ Clown
- ☐ Count Dracula
- ☐ Crown
- ☐ Drum
- ☐ Duck
- ☐ Fish (2)
- ☐ Flowerpot
- ☐ Giraffe
- ☐ Graduate
- ☐ Helmet
- ☐ Jack-in-the-box
- ☐ Key
- ☐ Lion
- ☐ Mirror
- ☐ Palm tree
- ☐ Pig
- ☐ Ring
- ☐ Sailboat
- ☐ Sailor's hat
- ☐ Sled
- ☐ Snake
- ☐ Stars (5)
- ☐ Toothbrush
- ☐ Truck
- ☐ Whale

What did Houdini do in Australia? Where is the rabbit going?

Lisa has finally made it! She's back home with all of her "Where Are They?" friends.

LOOK FOR LISA AND...

- ☐ Bats (2)
- ☐ Bones (2)
- ☐ Clouds (3)
- ☐ Gift
- ☐ Hammers (2)
- ☐ Hearts (3)
- ☐ Hose
- ☐ Oar
- ☐ Octopus
- ☐ Question mark
- ☐ Stars (5)
- ☐ Sunglasses (3)
- ☐ Tulip
- ☐ Turtle
- ☐ Watering can

Who knew where Lisa was?

LOOK FOR LISA

SEARCH FOR SYLVESTER

Sylvester has run out of bamboo shoots to eat, but the mall should be the perfect place to buy some more.

SEARCH FOR SYLVESTER AT THIS MAD MALL AND...

- ☐ Banana peel
- ☐ Bird
- ☐ Birdhouse
- ☐ Bow and arrow
- ☐ Bowling ball
- ☐ Bride
- ☐ Cactus
- ☐ Convict
- ☐ Crown
- ☐ Dog
- ☐ Dracula
- ☐ Drum
- ☐ Feathers (2)
- ☐ Fish (2)
- ☐ Football
- ☐ Heart
- ☐ Ice-cream cone
- ☐ Jack-in-the-box
- ☐ Jack-o´-lantern
- ☐ Lion
- ☐ Moose
- ☐ Pig
- ☐ Rabbit
- ☐ Sailboat
- ☐ Santa Claus
- ☐ Star
- ☐ Surfboard
- ☐ Toy panda
- ☐ Trumpet
- ☐ Tuba
- ☐ Turtle
- ☐ Umbrella

Sylvester had no luck at the mall, so he figured he'd try the park next. Boy, was he getting hungry!

SEARCH FOR SYLVESTER IN THIS FUN-FILLED PLAYGROUND AND…

☐ Artist's model
☐ Balloons (3)
☐ Baseball cap
☐ Birds (4)
☐ Cactus
☐ Cat
☐ Chef's hat
☐ Clipboard
☐ Crown
☐ Drum
☐ Ducklings (4)
☐ Fish
☐ Fisherman
☐ Fork
☐ Genie
☐ Graduate
☐ Hammer
☐ Heart
☐ Mailbox
☐ Mouse
☐ Paintbrush
☐ Pencils (2)
☐ Postal carrier
☐ Rabbit
☐ Roller skates
☐ Saddle
☐ Sailboats (2)
☐ Saws (2)
☐ Scooter
☐ Squirrel
☐ Sunglasses
☐ Top hat
☐ Trash basket
☐ Umbrella

What's for rent?
What's the price of a pickle?

There were no bamboo shoots in the park, so Sylvester stopped off at a place where they serve almost anything!

SEARCH FOR SYLVESTER AT FAST FOOD HEAVEN AND...

☐ Arrows (2)
☐ Bone
☐ Cactus
☐ Cane
☐ Chef
☐ Crocodile
☐ Dogs (2)
☐ Drummer
☐ Earmuffs
☐ Elephants (2)
☐ Flying bat
☐ Flying carpet
☐ Flying saucer
☐ Fork
☐ Gas mask
☐ Ghosts (2)
☐ Green balloons (3)
☐ Igloo
☐ Kangaroo
☐ King
☐ Knight
☐ Lion
☐ Net
☐ Octopus
☐ Owl
☐ Pig
☐ Queen
☐ Santa Claus
☐ Skunk
☐ Squirrel
☐ Top hat
☐ Tuba
☐ Turtle
☐ Viking

Who hopes that the fish is fresh?

"The zoo should have bamboo shoots," thought Sylvester after he failed to find any at FAST FOOD HEAVEN. So off he went.

SEARCH FOR SYLVESTER AT THE ZANY ZOO AND…

☐ Artist
☐ Balloon
☐ Basket
☐ Bat and ball
☐ Bear
☐ Birds (2)
☐ Brooms (2)
☐ Buzzard
☐ Candy cane
☐ Cook
☐ Crown
☐ Dracula
☐ Duck
☐ Flamingo
☐ Graduate
☐ Ice-cream cones (2)
☐ Key
☐ Monkey
☐ Mouse
☐ Painted egg
☐ Pencils (2)
☐ Penguin
☐ "Polly"
☐ Rabbit
☐ Rooster
☐ Sailboat
☐ Seahorse
☐ Spoon
☐ Toucan
☐ Toy ship

Who doesn't know?
Who is going back to Transylvania?

Sylvester had no luck finding bamboo shoots at the zoo, but his next stop is the ABCD school lunchroom. He's sure to find bamboo shoots there.

SEARCH FOR SYLVESTER IN THIS ALPHABETICAL SCHOOL AND...

- ☐ A
- ☐ B
- ☐ C
- ☐ D
- ☐ E
- ☐ F
- ☐ G
- ☐ H
- ☐ I
- ☐ J
- ☐ K
- ☐ L
- ☐ M
- ☐ N
- ☐ O
- ☐ P
- ☐ Q
- ☐ R
- ☐ S
- ☐ T
- ☐ U
- ☐ V
- ☐ W
- ☐ X
- ☐ Y
- ☐ Z
- ☐ Baseball cap
- ☐ Eyeglasses
- ☐ Spoon

What kind of prehistoric animal is it?

They were not serving bamboo shoots for lunch, but as Sylvester was leaving he heard cheering coming from the gym. "Maybe, they're selling bamboo shoots in there," he thought.

SEARCH FOR SYLVESTER AT THE BASKETBALL GAME AND...

☐ Baskets (2)
☐ Bird
☐ Bone
☐ Book
☐ Bunny
☐ Cleats
☐ Clown
☐ Dogs (2)
☐ Doughnut
☐ Elephant
☐ Envelopes (2)
☐ Fish
☐ Flower
☐ Football
☐ Frog
☐ Glove
☐ Horn
☐ Ice skate
☐ Ice-cream cone
☐ Juggler
☐ Mouse
☐ Necktie
☐ Popcorn
☐ Roller skates
☐ Sailor's cap
☐ Saw
☐ Slice of pizza
☐ Snake
☐ Stars (3)
☐ Toy arrow
☐ Whistle

Who wants to play, too?
Who is winning?

Not a single bamboo shoot was sold at the game. Sylvester was starving. He passed an old haunted house where someone was cooking. Could they be making bamboo shoots?

SEARCH FOR SYLVESTER AT THIS SPOOKY MANSION AND...

- ☐ Apple
- ☐ Arrows (2)
- ☐ Banana
- ☐ Bone
- ☐ Button
- ☐ Can
- ☐ Cook
- ☐ Cup
- ☐ Cupcake
- ☐ Fire hydrant
- ☐ Flashlight
- ☐ Flowerpot
- ☐ Heart
- ☐ Ice-cream soda
- ☐ Jack-o´-lantern
- ☐ Keyboard
- ☐ Kite
- ☐ Mask
- ☐ Medal
- ☐ Old shoe
- ☐ Pencil
- ☐ Pie
- ☐ Pot
- ☐ Rat
- ☐ Ring
- ☐ Skateboard
- ☐ Skulls (2)
- ☐ Sled
- ☐ Street light
- ☐ Sword
- ☐ Swordfish
- ☐ Trash can
- ☐ Turtle
- ☐ Umbrella

Sylvester didn't enter the haunted house, and now he was really, really hungry. "Maybe Detective Donald can help me detect bamboo shoots," thought Sylvester.

SEARCH FOR SYLVESTER AT DETECTIVE DONALD'S DIGS AND…

- ☐ Apple core
- ☐ Beard and glasses disguise
- ☐ Blackboard
- ☐ Bomb
- ☐ Boot
- ☐ Broken legs (2)
- ☐ Broken pencils (3)
- ☐ Buckets (2)
- ☐ Candles (3)
- ☐ Cupcake
- ☐ Dart
- ☐ Deflated balloon
- ☐ Dumbbell
- ☐ Eraser
- ☐ Feather
- ☐ Fish
- ☐ Fly swatter
- ☐ Footprints
- ☐ Graduation cap
- ☐ Hamburger
- ☐ Hockey stick
- ☐ Hole in a shoe
- ☐ Hooks (3)
- ☐ Hourglass
- ☐ Ink bottle
- ☐ Mirror
- ☐ Mouse
- ☐ Owl
- ☐ Paintbrush
- ☐ Record
- ☐ Ring
- ☐ Roller skate
- ☐ Slice of pizza
- ☐ Stars (3)

Detective Donald advised Sylvester to look under the big top for bamboo shoots.

SEARCH FOR
SYLVESTER
AT THIS SILLY
CIRCUS AND...

☐ Baker
☐ Banana
☐ Bat
☐ Bearded man
☐ Binoculars
☐ Candy cane
☐ Carrot
☐ Clothespins (3)
☐ Cup
☐ Dog
☐ Elephants (2)
☐ Feather
☐ Fire hydrant
☐ Giraffe
☐ Hot dog
☐ Humpty Dumpty
☐ Ice skates
☐ Ice-cream cone
☐ Kangaroo
☐ Lamp
☐ Mice (2)
☐ Mother Goose
☐ Paint bucket
☐ Paper bag
☐ Periscope
☐ Pig
☐ Pillow
☐ Rabbit
☐ Seals (2)
☐ Skunk
☐ Slice of watermelon
☐ Stars (5)
☐ Top hat
☐ Turtle
☐ Umbrella
☐ Unicorn
☐ Watering can
☐ Wizard

Who lost his costume?

Sylvester had no luck at the circus, but on his way home he spotted a hot air balloon about to take off. "From up there I'll be able to find bamboo shoots," thought Sylvester.

SEARCH FOR SYLVESTER AS HE SOARS THROUGH THE SKY AND...

☐ Alien spaceship
☐ Ape
☐ Apple
☐ Arrows (2)
☐ Books (2)
☐ Bowling balls (2)
☐ Broom
☐ Candy canes (2)
☐ Chef
☐ Clowns (2)
☐ Coffeepot
☐ Cup
☐ Ducks (2)
☐ Firecracker
☐ Fish (2)
☐ Fishing pole
☐ Flowerpot
☐ Footballs (2)
☐ Hearts (2)
☐ Horns (2)
☐ Hose
☐ Hot dog
☐ Light bulb
☐ Lips
☐ Magnifying
   glasses (2)
☐ Painted eggs (2)
☐ Pencil
☐ Pillow
☐ Slices of
   watermelon (2)
☐ Telescopes (2)
☐ Tires (2)
☐ Turtles (2)

Who is the witch talking to?

From way up above Sylvester saw his old neighborhood. "That's it!" thought Sylvester. "I should have known to go back home to mom."

SEARCH FOR SYLVESTER IN BAMBOO TOWN AND...

☐ Apple
☐ Artist
☐ Backpack
☐ Birds (3)
☐ Bone
☐ Bucket
☐ Cactus
☐ Cash register
☐ Cat
☐ Crowns (2)
☐ Dogs (2)
☐ Elephant
☐ Feather
☐ Fish (3)
☐ Hammer
☐ Hoe
☐ Key
☐ Kiddie pool
☐ Mailbox
☐ Mushroom
☐ Photographer
☐ Pie
☐ Pitcher
☐ Pitchfork
☐ Pumpkin
☐ Scarecrow
☐ Scissors
☐ Scooter
☐ Screwdriver
☐ Sword
☐ Tricycle
☐ Turtles (2)
☐ Umbrella

What is the name of the street?
Who is "Captain Bamboo"?

Sylvester ate all the bamboo shoots he wanted yesterday, but today he woke up hungry again!

SEARCH FOR SYLVESTER AND…

☐ Candy cane
☐ Envelope
☐ Flamingo
☐ Flying bat
☐ Hearts (2)
☐ Horseshoe
☐ Light bulb
☐ Mushroom
☐ Musical notes (2)
☐ Painted eggs (2)
☐ Picture
☐ Pitcher
☐ Raccoon
☐ Stars (2)

SEARCH FOR SYLVESTER

Wendy is a typical teenager—with one small difference—she's a witch. Like other kids her age, she attends school. *Unlike* other kids her age, she attends a very special school—a school for witches!

FIND WENDY AT WITCHVILLE HIGH SCHOOL AND...

- ☐ Arrow
- ☑ Balloon
- ☐ Bear
- ☐ Blue-eyed monster
- ☐ Bones (3)
- ☐ Book
- ☐ Broken window
- ☐ Brooms (6)
- ☐ Candle
- ☐ Candy cane
- ☐ Costume
- ☐ Elephant
- ☐ Fish (3)
- ☐ Fishbowl
- ☐ Green-eyed monster
- ☐ Horseshoe
- ☐ Kettles (2)
- ☐ Key
- ☐ Kites (2)
- ☐ Lost shoe
- ☐ Mummy
- ☐ Mushrooms (3)
- ☐ Owl
- ☐ Pig
- ☐ Principal
- ☐ Pumpkin
- ☐ Question-mark hat
- ☐ Rabbit
- ☐ Schoolbag
- ☐ Skulls (3)
- ☐ Snake
- ☐ Star
- ☐ "Thirteen" (3)

What is the cobweb collection for?
What time do classes start?

It's another typical day at Witchville High. In this class the young witches are learning their witchcraft. However, Wendy doesn't seem too interested in learning how to be a witch.

LOOK FOR WENDY IN THE CLASSROOM AND...

☐ Apples (2)
☐ Axe
☐ Banana peel
☐ Baseball
☐ Bow
☐ Broken mirror
☐ Brooms (3)
☐ Bugs (2)
☐ Candles (3)
☐ Cupcake
☐ Dead flowers
☐ Fish
☐ Flower
☐ Flying bats (2)
☐ Ghost
☐ Hamburger
☐ Hammer
☐ Heart
☐ Hourglass
☐ Ice skates
☐ Marshmallow
☐ Mouse
☐ Octopus
☐ Paper airplane
☐ Roller skates
☐ Scissors
☐ Screwdriver
☐ Ski
☐ Skulls (3)
☐ Skunk
☐ Snake
☐ Spool of thread
☐ Turtle
☐ Worm

What time is it?
Which witch drew
the picture?

Hooray!! It's class trip day! Where are Wendy and her witchy friends going? To a haunted house, of course!

SEARCH FOR WENDY ON THE WITCHES' CLASS TRIP AND...

☐ Apple
☐ Basket
☐ Basketball
☐ Bird
☐ Bones (2)
☐ Cactus
☐ Candle
☐ Chair
☐ Chicken
☐ Crayon
☐ Crocodile
☐ Dogs (2)
☐ Faucet
☐ Flowers (2)
☐ Flying bat
☐ Football
☐ Ghost
☐ Hearts (2)
☐ Hockey stick
☐ Hot dogs (2)
☐ Ice-cream cone
☐ Ice skate
☐ Mitten
☐ Mouse
☐ Paintbrush
☐ Paint bucket
☐ Painted egg
☐ Periscope
☐ Pizza slice
☐ Sailor cap
☐ Saw
☐ Skulls (2)
☐ Squirrel
☐ Sunglasses (2)
☐ Tombstone
☐ Top hat
☐ Turtles (3)
☐ Watermelon slice

Which witch had her hair done?

Wendy's favorite time of day is lunch time. The food at Witchville High is not too different from the food at most schools.

FIND WENDY IN THE LUNCHROOM AND...

- ☐ Banana peel
- ☐ Bat
- ☐ Black cat
- ☐ Bone
- ☐ Books (2)
- ☐ Bowling ball
- ☐ Brooms (2)
- ☐ Chef's hat
- ☐ Clothespin
- ☐ Crown
- ☐ Crystal ball
- ☐ Empty bowl
- ☐ Eyeglasses
- ☐ Feather
- ☐ Fish (2)
- ☐ Fork
- ☐ Frog
- ☐ Ghost
- ☐ Graduate
- ☐ Hatched egg
- ☐ Ice skate
- ☐ Mouse
- ☐ Musicians (4)
- ☐ Necktie
- ☐ Pig
- ☐ Rabbits (2)
- ☐ Radio
- ☐ Sailor cap
- ☐ Snakes (2)
- ☐ Sock
- ☐ "Spot"
- ☐ Straw hat
- ☐ Sunglasses
- ☐ Tea kettle
- ☐ Trash can
- ☐ Waiter

Which witch has a bandage?
Which witch has a bow?

Final exams are lots of fun with this bunch of wacky witches! Wendy is happy just watching her classmates displaying their witchy ways.

LOOK FOR WENDY DURING FINAL EXAMS AND...

- ☐ Apples (5)
- ☐ Baseball bat
- ☐ Bell
- ☐ Bird
- ☐ Birdcage
- ☐ Bones (5)
- ☐ Book
- ☐ Candles (2)
- ☐ Cat
- ☐ Clipboards (4)
- ☐ Fish (2)
- ☐ Flower
- ☐ Hose
- ☐ Ice-cream cone
- ☐ Kite
- ☐ Lock
- ☐ Mitten
- ☐ Necklace
- ☐ Owl
- ☐ Painted egg
- ☐ Pear
- ☐ Periscope
- ☐ Pillow
- ☐ Pogo stick
- ☐ Purse
- ☐ Roller skates
- ☐ Sailboat
- ☐ Skis
- ☐ Skulls (2)
- ☐ Snake
- ☐ Soccer ball
- ☐ Telephone
- ☐ Umbrella
- ☐ Watering can
- ☐ Witch doctor

Which witch can make her hair stand up?
Which witch has an apple?

Graduation day has finally arrived. Now all these fine young witches will start looking for witches' work. Wendy wonders what her first job will be.

HUNT FOR WENDY AT GRADUATION AND...

- ☐ Arrow
- ☐ Balloons (4)
- ☐ Banana peel
- ☐ Bomb
- ☐ Cane
- ☐ Eyeglasses
- ☐ Firecrackers (2)
- ☐ Fish
- ☐ Flying bats (2)
- ☐ Hearts (3)
- ☐ Hot dog
- ☐ Humpty Dumpty
- ☐ Ice-cream pop
- ☐ Ice skates
- ☐ Igloo
- ☐ Leaping lizard
- ☐ Mailbox
- ☐ Manhole cover
- ☐ Mary Poppins
- ☐ Misplaced flowerpot
- ☐ Mouse
- ☐ Paint bucket
- ☐ Panda
- ☐ Periscope
- ☐ Pie
- ☐ Pillow
- ☐ Pizza
- ☐ Pumpkins (2)
- ☐ Record
- ☐ Robot
- ☐ Sleeping witches (2)
- ☐ Stocking cap
- ☐ Tepee
- ☐ Turtle
- ☐ Vulture
- ☐ Worm

Who is the school dropout?
Who wasn't invited?

Wendy gets a job at the Count's castle. What is she doing?!? Instead of witching around, she's cleaning! The Count and his creepy friends are not happy. Better look for work someplace else, Wendy.

FIND WENDY IN COUNT DRACULA'S LIVING ROOM AND...

☐ Apple
☐ Bones (2)
☐ Brooms (3)
☐ Candles (2)
☐ Candy cane
☐ Dog
☐ Fish
☐ Flying bats (5)
☐ Football
☐ Ghosts (2)
☐ Globe
☐ Hearts (3)
☐ Hot dog
☐ Ice skate
☐ One-eyed monster
☐ Painted egg
☐ Palm tree
☐ Piano keys
☐ Pick
☐ Quarter moons (2)
☐ Skull
☐ Snail
☐ Star
☐ Straw
☐ Tombstones (2)
☐ Tulip
☐ Umbrellas (3)
☐ Wreath
☐ Yo-Yo

What is Dracula's favorite fruit?
Where did the flowers come from?
Who is moving to the Vampire State Building?

Wendy's next job is assisting Dr. Frankenstein. She's cleaned and organized his laboratory, and spruced up Frankenstein's monster! She probably won't last too long here, either.

SEARCH FOR WENDY IN DR. FRANKENSTEIN'S LABORATORY AND...

☐ Apple
☐ Baseball
☐ Bell
☐ Bone
☐ Book
☐ Cactus
☐ Candy cane
☐ Dancer
☐ Fish
☐ Flowers (2)
☐ Flying bat
☐ Ghost
☐ Hat
☐ Mice (4)
☐ Music notes (4)
☐ Oil can
☐ Pear
☐ Pencil
☐ Pillow
☐ Roller skates
☐ Screwdriver
☐ Skulls (2)
☐ Snake
☐ Socks (3)
☐ Speakers (2)
☐ Straw
☐ Suspenders (2 pairs)
☐ Tick-tack-toe
☐ Toast
☐ Vulture
☐ Welcome mat

How high can the monster jump?
What did Fritz drop?

Wendy finds another job —in a mummy's tomb! She decides to redecorate the tomb with plants and flowers. However, the mummy is not amused. In fact, he's very upset! Wendy has done it again. She just can't behave in a witchlike way.

HUNT FOR WENDY IN THE MUMMY'S TOMB AND...

☐ Airplane
☐ Award
☐ Bell
☐ Bird
☐ Butterfly
☐ Clown
☐ Duck
☐ Elephant
☐ Fish
☐ Hammer
☐ Heart
☐ Hose
☐ Ice-cream cone
☐ Ice skate
☐ Key
☐ Kite
☐ Lion
☐ Lobster
☐ Mushroom
☐ Necktie
☐ Painted egg
☐ Quarter moon
☐ Rabbit
☐ Ring
☐ Rooster
☐ Sailboat
☐ Sea horse
☐ Seal
☐ Snowman
☐ Sock
☐ Starfish
☐ Tepee
☐ Tiger
☐ Umbrella
☐ Worm

Who wants a peanut?

The witches have found the perfect job for Wendy! The next time you see a jack-o'-lantern, think of Wendy growing them on her farm.

FIND WENDY ON THE JACK-O'-LANTERN FARM AND...

☐ Apple
☐ Baseball bat
☐ Birds (2)
☐ Bones (2)
☐ Bowling ball
☐ Cactus
☐ Carrot
☐ Duck
☐ Egg
☐ Fat candle
☐ Fire hydrant
☐ Flashlight
☐ Frog
☐ Ghosts (2)
☐ Hoe
☐ Kangaroo
☐ Lawn mower
☐ Lollipop
☐ Lost boot
☐ Magnifying glass
☐ Mailbox
☐ Mask
☐ Mummy
☐ Paper bag
☐ Pear
☐ Periscope
☐ Pig
☐ Rake
☐ Roller skates
☐ Skulls (2)
☐ Skunk
☐ Surfboard

What's for rent?
What's sleeping?
Who drinks lemon juice?
Who works for Wendy?
Who's afraid?

All of Wendy's "Where Are They?" friends have come to visit her jack-o'-lantern farm.

LOOK FOR:

☐ Bone
☐ Boot
☐ Brooms (3)
☐ Canes (2)
☐ Chicken
☐ Crayon
☐ Flowers (2)
☐ Heart
☐ Mouse
☐ Mushroom
☐ Nail
☐ Smallest jack-o'-lantern

WHERE'S WENDY?

WHERE ARE THEY?

GROSS STUFF

CRYPTS
MADE WHILE-U-WAIT.

DID YOU
DO YOUR
HOMEWORK?

I'LL BE
HOME FO
BREAKFA

FIND FREDDIE & LISA IN THE HAUNTED HOUSE

Spook yourself silly in the haunted house
looking for Freddie and Lisa.

Search through the creepy castle.

Find Frankie and his monster friends.

Experience monster madness!

MONSTER MADNESS

CREEPY CASTLE

FIND FRANKIE & HIS MONSTER FRIENDS

STANT
UD!

FIND FREDDIE & LISA

IN THE

HAUNTED HOUSE

Freddie and Lisa have discovered a house that's unlike any other...a haunted house!

FIND FREDDIE & LISA AT THE HAUNTED HOUSE AND...

- ☐ Apples (2)
- ☐ Apron
- ☐ Baseball cap
- ☐ Bats (2)
- ☐ Bones (3)
- ☐ Box
- ☐ Burned-out candle
- ☐ Clothespin
- ☐ Coffeepot
- ☐ Crown
- ☐ Dog
- ☐ Dracula
- ☐ Duck
- ☐ Eyeglasses
- ☐ Faucet
- ☐ Fish tank
- ☐ Fishing pole
- ☐ Ghosts (3)
- ☐ Hammer
- ☐ Heart
- ☐ Kite
- ☐ Light bulb
- ☐ Lips
- ☐ Mouse
- ☐ Mummy
- ☐ Owl
- ☐ Paint bucket
- ☐ Paper bag
- ☐ Peanut
- ☐ Pencils (2)
- ☐ Piggy bank
- ☐ Question mark
- ☐ Saw
- ☐ Scarves (2)
- ☐ Sock
- ☐ Straw
- ☐ Submarine
- ☐ Tire
- ☐ Truck
- ☐ Umbrella

Should they go in?
Should they not go in?
What do you think
they should do?

FIND FREDDIE &
LISA BEFORE
THEY DECIDE
AND...

- ☐ Birds (2)
- ☐ Black paint
- ☐ Blimps (2)
- ☐ Bowling ball
- ☐ Box
- ☐ Broom
- ☐ Burned-out bulb
- ☐ Cactus
- ☐ Camel
- ☐ Candle
- ☐ Chef's hat
- ☐ Feather
- ☐ Flower
- ☐ Football
- ☐ Giant straw
- ☐ Giraffe
- ☐ Jester
- ☐ King
- ☐ Laundry
- ☐ License plate
- ☐ Longest hair
- ☐ Lost boot
- ☐ Lost mask
- ☐ Mustache
- ☐ Napoleon
- ☐ Painted egg
- ☐ Rabbit
- ☐ Rain cloud
- ☐ Red wagon
- ☐ Sailboat
- ☐ Short pants
- ☐ Skull
- ☐ Sled
- ☐ Slide
- ☐ Star
- ☐ Top hats (2)
- ☐ Trash can
- ☐ Umbrella
- ☐ Who can't go?

Ready...Set...Go!!
Everyone runs toward
the door of the haunted
house...but only
two enter!

FIND FREDDIE &
LISA AS THEY
MEET THE
MONSTERS AND...

- ☐ Apple
- ☐ Arrow
- ☐ Bag
- ☐ Balloon
- ☐ Banana peel
- ☐ Baseball cap
- ☐ Bodiless head
- ☐ Bone
- ☐ Boot
- ☐ Bows (3)
- ☐ Broken heart
- ☐ Broom
- ☐ Cake
- ☐ Can
- ☐ Candles (5)
- ☐ Clothesline
- ☐ Crystal ball
- ☐ Earrings
- ☐ Eyeglasses
- ☐ Fish
- ☐ Flower
- ☐ Four-eyed monster
- ☐ Genie
- ☐ Ghosts (2)
- ☐ Ice-cream cone
- ☐ Lightning
- ☐ Necktie
- ☐ Number 13
- ☐ Owl
- ☐ Piano
- ☐ Roller skates
- ☐ Santa Claus
- ☐ Six-fingered hand
- ☐ Skulls (5)
- ☐ Snake
- ☐ Spoon
- ☐ Tombstone
- ☐ Watering can
- ☐ Worms (2)

Ms. Witch makes monstrous snacks. Her specialty is the "Everything Goes" sandwich!

FIND FREDDIE & LISA AT SNACK TIME AND...

☐ Accordion
☐ Apple
☐ Baseball
☐ Bell
☐ Blackbird
☐ Bone
☐ Brush
☐ Candle
☐ Checkerboard
☐ Drill
☐ Earring
☐ Faucet
☐ Fish (2)
☐ Flower
☐ Fork
☐ Frying pan
☐ Grapes
☐ Green cup
☐ Heart
☐ Helmet
☐ Ice-cream cone
☐ Ladle
☐ Mustaches (2)
☐ Neckties (2)
☐ Oil can
☐ Orange
☐ Palm tree
☐ Pear
☐ Polka-dotted
    handkerchief
☐ Rolling pin
☐ Saw
☐ Scissors
☐ Sock
☐ Stool
☐ Straw
☐ Toaster
☐ TV set
☐ Watermelon
☐ Wooden spoon

Freddie & Lisa begin to explore the haunted house. A wrong turn and...down, down, down they tumble.

FIND FREDDIE & LISA IN THE DUNGEON AND...

☐ Airplane
☐ Balloon
☐ Banana peel
☐ Bomb
☐ Book
☐ Bowling ball
☐ Broken egg
☐ Broom
☐ Candy cane
☐ Corn
☐ Cupcake
☐ Doctor
☐ Drum
☐ Fire hydrant
☐ Flowerpot
☐ Flying bat
☐ Football
☐ Hammer
☐ Hot dog
☐ Ice-cream cone
☐ Ice-cream pop
☐ Mummies (3)
☐ Piggy bank
☐ Rabbit
☐ Racer
☐ Roller skates
☐ Scarecrow
☐ School bag
☐ Shark
☐ Showerhead
☐ Skateboard
☐ Skulls (2)
☐ Skunk
☐ Sock
☐ Star
☐ Swing
☐ Top hat
☐ Trash can
☐ Trumpet
☐ Umbrellas (2)
☐ Wagon

Next to the dungeon are the wildest lanes in town. It's a great place to do anything—but bowl!

FIND FREDDIE & LISA AT THE GHOSTLY BOWLING ALLEY AND...

- ☐ Arrow
- ☐ Balloon
- ☐ Bat
- ☐ Bird
- ☐ Bodiless head
- ☐ Bomb
- ☐ Boom box
- ☐ Broken ball
- ☐ Broom
- ☐ Cactus
- ☐ Candles (2)
- ☐ Carrot
- ☐ Delivery creature
- ☐ Dog
- ☐ Earphones
- ☐ Flower
- ☐ Hamburger
- ☐ Hot dog
- ☐ Humpty Dumpty
- ☐ Mouse
- ☐ Mummy
- ☐ Mummy's ball
- ☐ Orange
- ☐ Pear
- ☐ Pennant
- ☐ Periscope
- ☐ Rabbit
- ☐ Robot
- ☐ Sailboat
- ☐ Skull
- ☐ Snowman
- ☐ Spring
- ☐ Square ball
- ☐ Sunglasses (2 pairs)
- ☐ Sword
- ☐ Tennis racket
- ☐ Tombstone
- ☐ Watermelon slice
- ☐ Who quit?
- ☐ Who ordered pizza?
- ☐ Worm
- ☐ Yo-yo

Dr. Frankenstein has lots of patients who need lots of patience.

FIND FREDDIE & LISA IN DR. FRANKENSTEIN'S LABORATORY AND...

- ☐ Black cat
- ☐ Book
- ☐ Bow tie
- ☐ Bride
- ☐ Bunny fiend
- ☐ Candle
- ☐ Cheese
- ☐ Dog
- ☐ Dracula
- ☐ Duck
- ☐ Feather
- ☐ Greeting card
- ☐ Hot hat
- ☐ Ice-cream pop
- ☐ Invisible person
- ☐ Neckerchief
- ☐ Paintbrush
- ☐ Paint bucket
- ☐ Pickax
- ☐ Roller skates
- ☐ Sailor fiend
- ☐ Saw
- ☐ Screwdriver
- ☐ Shovel
- ☐ Skull
- ☐ Suspenders
- ☐ Thing-in-a-sack
- ☐ Three-eyed creature
- ☐ Three-legged thing
- ☐ Toothbrush
- ☐ Tulip
- ☐ TV set
- ☐ Two-headed thing
- ☐ Watch
- ☐ Who has a sore throat?
- ☐ Who has a toothache?
- ☐ Who needs a haircut?
- ☐ Who snores?
- ☐ Who's been shrunk?
- ☐ Who's on a diet?
- ☐ Wooden block

After dinner, Freddie and Lisa explore a junk-filled room upstairs. There they find someone who <u>really</u> knows how to save!

FIND FREDDIE & LISA IN DRACULA'S ATTIC AND...

- ☐ Book
- ☐ Boomerang
- ☐ Broom
- ☐ Calendar
- ☐ Candy cane
- ☐ Chef's hat
- ☐ Clocks (2)
- ☐ Cracked mirror
- ☐ Fire hydrant
- ☐ Garden hose
- ☐ Golf club
- ☐ Ice-cream cone
- ☐ Key
- ☐ Moon
- ☐ Mouse
- ☐ Necklace
- ☐ Necktie
- ☐ Oar
- ☐ Old-fashioned radio
- ☐ Paint bucket
- ☐ Paper airplane
- ☐ Pencil
- ☐ Pyramid
- ☐ Santa's hat
- ☐ Saw
- ☐ Skateboard
- ☐ Skulls (4)
- ☐ Slice of pizza
- ☐ Spray can
- ☐ Stocking
- ☐ Straw
- ☐ String of pearls
- ☐ Stuffed panda
- ☐ Target
- ☐ Telephone booth
- ☐ Top hat
- ☐ Train engine
- ☐ Viking helmet
- ☐ Wagon wheel
- ☐ Wig
- ☐ Yarn

The monsters walk very carefully when they visit this room!

FIND FREDDIE & LISA IN THE COBWEB ROOM AND...

- ☐ Baby carriage
- ☐ Bats (2)
- ☐ Binoculars
- ☐ Boot
- ☐ Bow tie
- ☐ Boxing glove
- ☐ Broom
- ☐ Cup
- ☐ Dog
- ☐ Duck
- ☐ Earring
- ☐ Electric plug
- ☐ Fish
- ☐ Flower
- ☐ Football helmet
- ☐ Fork
- ☐ Ghosts (2)
- ☐ Hammer
- ☐ Heart
- ☐ Key
- ☐ Kite
- ☐ Lock
- ☐ Moon face
- ☐ Mummy
- ☐ Number 13
- ☐ Old-fashioned radio
- ☐ Paintbrush
- ☐ Pencil
- ☐ Ring
- ☐ Robot
- ☐ Screwdriver
- ☐ Ship
- ☐ Six-fingered creature
- ☐ Skull
- ☐ Spider
- ☐ Top hat
- ☐ Train engine
- ☐ Turtles (2)
- ☐ Umbrella
- ☐ Wagon

FIND FREDDIE & LISA IN THE MONSTERS' PLAYROOM AND...

- ☐ Artist
- ☐ Balloon
- ☐ Banana peel
- ☐ Barbell
- ☐ Beanie
- ☐ Birds (2)
- ☐ Blackboard
- ☐ Crayons (5)
- ☐ Donkey
- ☐ Fish
- ☐ Football
- ☐ Haunted house
- ☐ Hole in the head
- ☐ Hood
- ☐ Ice skate
- ☐ Jack-o'-lanterns (4)
- ☐ Jacks (4)
- ☐ Joke book
- ☐ Juggler
- ☐ Loose change
- ☐ Mask
- ☐ Monster-in-the-box
- ☐ Monster puppet
- ☐ Mummy doll
- ☐ Musician
- ☐ Nail
- ☐ Pail
- ☐ "Pin-the-tail-on-the-donkey"
- ☐ Pogo stick
- ☐ Rubber ducky
- ☐ Sailboat
- ☐ Snake
- ☐ Telephone
- ☐ Tepee
- ☐ Three-legged thing
- ☐ Tricycle
- ☐ Truck
- ☐ Turtle
- ☐ TV set
- ☐ Who attends "Horror U"?
- ☐ Wind-up monster

It's time for Freddie & Lisa to go. The friendly monsters hope their new friends will return soon.

FIND FREDDIE & LISA LEAVING THE HAUNTED HOUSE AND...

- ☐ Apple
- ☐ Arrow
- ☐ Balloon
- ☐ Birds (2)
- ☐ Box
- ☐ Broken heart
- ☐ Brooms (2)
- ☐ Candles (2)
- ☐ Clock
- ☐ Crown
- ☐ Did they have fun?
- ☐ Dog
- ☐ Duck
- ☐ Envelope
- ☐ Feather
- ☐ Firecracker
- ☐ Flower
- ☐ Ice skates
- ☐ Jack-o'-lanterns (4)
- ☐ Key
- ☐ Ladder
- ☐ Lamp
- ☐ Moon face
- ☐ Mouse
- ☐ Painted egg
- ☐ Periscope
- ☐ Rabbit
- ☐ Roller skates
- ☐ Scarves (3)
- ☐ Seven-fingered creature
- ☐ Shovel
- ☐ Skull
- ☐ Straw
- ☐ Tick-Tack-Toe
- ☐ Top hat
- ☐ Tree
- ☐ TV camera
- ☐ Umbrella
- ☐ When will they return?
- ☐ Which exit did they use?
- ☐ Who will miss them the most?
- ☐ Who doesn't use toothpaste?

Freddie and Lisa are
here with a few of their
playmates.

Donald   Hector
Frankie   Susie
Laura   Bunny Honey
Sam   Santa
Santa's helpers — Fee, Fi, Fo and Fun

MONSTER MADNESS

There once was an ancient house, in an ancient part of town, that was discovered by two not so ancient children. They wanted to go inside, but first they had to find the following hidden pictures. Can you help them?

☐ Banana
☐ Bone
☐ Book
☐ Boot
☐ Bottle
☐ Broom
☐ Carrot
☐ Elephant
☐ Envelope
☐ Fish
☐ Flower
☐ Flying bat
☐ Fork
☐ Guitar

☐ Hairbrush
☐ Hammer
☐ Heart
☐ Hockey stick
☐ Horseshoe
☐ Hot dog
☐ Kitchen knife
☐ Lost wallet
☐ Owl
☐ Palm tree
☐ Pencil
☐ Question mark

☐ Rabbit
☐ Sailboat
☐ Saw
☐ Screwdriver
☐ Skull
☐ Snake
☐ Star
☐ Tepee
☐ Tick-tack-toe
☐ Toothbrush
☐ Top hat
☐ Zipper

WELCOME TO ANCIENT ACRES

WE FOUND IT! LET'S GO INSIDE!

NOT FOR SALE

In the ancient house, was an ancient truck, which was opened with an ancient key, by the not so ancient children. Out of the trunk came many strange things including the hidden objects below.

- ☐ Arrow
- ☐ Balloon
- ☐ Bearded man
- ☐ Carrot
- ☐ Chicken
- ☐ Clown
- ☐ Cow
- ☐ Elephant
- ☐ Envelope
- ☐ Fish

- ☐ Giraffe
- ☐ Horse
- ☐ Kite
- ☐ Moon face
- ☐ Mouse
- ☐ Pumpkin
- ☐ Rabbit
- ☐ Saw

- ☐ Snowman
- ☐ Tepee
- ☐ Tombstone
- ☐ Turtle
- ☐ Unicorn
- ☐ Watermelon slice
- ☐ Witch

Did you ever see such a sight in your life? No, it's not three blind mice—it's monsters, monsters, monsters! Monsters can be found everywhere along with the following hidden pictures. Can you find them all?

☐ Arrow
☐ Automobile
☐ Bell
☐ Bird
☐ Candle
☐ Candy canes (2)
☐ Clothespin
☐ Comb
☐ Drum
☐ Evergreen tree
☐ Fish
☐ Flower
☐ Football
☐ Fork

☐ Hairbrush
☐ Hot dog
☐ Kangaroo
☐ Key
☐ Locket
☐ Mouse
☐ Pen
☐ Pencil
☐ Scarf
☐ Skateboard
☐ Sock
☐ Star
☐ Tent
☐ Turtle
☐ Umbrella

In another ancient room in the ancient house the two kids found ... an ANCIENT FAMILY ALBUM! Whose pictures do you think were inside? Wait! Before you can open it, you must first find:

☐ Arrow
☐ Banana
☐ Bear
☐ Cactus
☐ Cane
☐ Cat
☐ Deer
☐ Duck
☐ Fork
☐ Frog
☐ Ghost
☐ Giraffe
☐ Goat
☐ Heart
☐ Hot dog
☐ Ice-cream cone

☐ Lamb
☐ Monkey
☐ Mouse
☐ Owl
☐ Pencil
☐ Pig
☐ Rabbit
☐ Ring
☐ Rooster
☐ Saw
☐ Skull
☐ Snake
☐ Squirrel
☐ Star
☐ Turtle

Wow! What a surprise! It's a photo album full of monsters! On the first page there's a picture of young Frankenstein on his first date. Do you know which monster is on the next page? Before you look, find the following hidden objects.

- ☐ Airplane
- ☐ Automobile
- ☐ Bomb
- ☐ Butterfly
- ☐ Camera
- ☐ Candle
- ☐ Cup
- ☐ Drum
- ☐ Eyeglasses
- ☐ Fish
- ☐ Hair bows (3)

- ☐ Hearts (4)
- ☐ House
- ☐ Kite
- ☐ Light bulb
- ☐ Owl
- ☐ Pencil
- ☐ Ring
- ☐ Rocket ship
- ☐ Sailboat

- ☐ Snake
- ☐ Surboard
- ☐ Sword
- ☐ Tent
- ☐ Toothbrush
- ☐ Tree
- ☐ Turtle
- ☐ Umbrella
- ☐ Whistle

Wasn't Count Dracuala a cuddly little critter? It is true … he was born with fangs! He also loved to hide things. Can you find everything he's hidden on this page?

- ☐ Arrow
- ☐ Carrot
- ☐ Clown
- ☐ Coffeepot
- ☐ Comb
- ☐ Crown
- ☐ Elephant
- ☐ Fish
- ☐ Flashlight
- ☐ Flower
- ☐ Flying bats (10)
- ☐ Football
- ☐ Ghost
- ☐ Heart
- ☐ Hockey stick
- ☐ Hot dog
- ☐ Ice-cream cone
- ☐ Igloo
- ☐ Jack-o'-lantern
- ☐ Key
- ☐ Kite
- ☐ Locomotive
- ☐ Mushroom
- ☐ Paintbrush
- ☐ Pencil
- ☐ Pizza
- ☐ Pyramid
- ☐ Sailor's hat
- ☐ Top hat
- ☐ Watermelon slice

This page has the largest picture in the monster family album. It's the abominable snow-kid building snow monsters. He's also thrown in some hidden pictures. Look closely to see if you can find them all.

- ☐ Alligator
- ☐ Banana
- ☐ Basket
- ☐ Bow tie
- ☐ Bowling ball
- ☐ Cactus
- ☐ Can
- ☐ Candle
- ☐ Candy cane
- ☐ Chair
- ☐ Cheese
- ☐ Chef's hat
- ☐ Cowboy hat
- ☐ Duck
- ☐ Fish
- ☐ Ghost
- ☐ Heart
- ☐ Hot dog
- ☐ Ice skate
- ☐ Ice-cream cone
- ☐ Ladder
- ☐ Lamp
- ☐ Lion
- ☐ Mouse
- ☐ Paintbrush
- ☐ Picture frame
- ☐ Pie
- ☐ Pig
- ☐ Pirate
- ☐ Shoe
- ☐ Shovel
- ☐ Top hat
- ☐ Umbrella
- ☐ Watering can
- ☐ Witch

Here's the mummy showing off his childhood pictures. You can certainly get wrapped up in them! You can also get wrapped up in looking for the following hidden objects.

- ☐ Apple
- ☐ Arrow
- ☐ Artist
- ☐ Bird
- ☐ Blimp
- ☐ Bone
- ☐ Book
- ☐ Broom
- ☐ Clothespin
- ☐ Cupcake
- ☐ Drum
- ☐ Envelope

- ☐ Fish
- ☐ Flying bat
- ☐ Football
- ☐ Ghost
- ☐ Golf club
- ☐ Hammer
- ☐ Kangaroo
- ☐ Kite
- ☐ Magnifying glass

- ☐ Owl
- ☐ Paintbrush
- ☐ Pinocchio
- ☐ Quarter moon
- ☐ Sailor's hat
- ☐ Saw
- ☐ Scarecrow
- ☐ Wagon

These are really terrific pictures ... the best in the album! They are, of course, pictures of the invisible man throughout the years. He is looking with you to find:

- ☐ Banana
- ☐ Basket
- ☐ Bone
- ☐ Candy cane
- ☐ Carrot
- ☐ Cheese
- ☐ Cupcake
- ☐ Evergreen tree
- ☐ Fire hydrant
- ☐ Football
- ☐ Graduation cap
- ☐ Guitar
- ☐ Hamburger
- ☐ Heart
- ☐ Hot dog
- ☐ Ice-cream soda
- ☐ Light bulb
- ☐ Monster-in-a-box
- ☐ Mouse
- ☐ Pear
- ☐ Pencil
- ☐ Rose
- ☐ Screwdriver
- ☐ Shovel
- ☐ Snail
- ☐ Star
- ☐ Tent
- ☐ Turtle
- ☐ TV set
- ☐ Unicorn

FIRST BIRTHDAY ↵

KID LEAGUE STAR ↵

FIRST DAY OF SCHOOL ↵

INVISIBLE PAPER ↵

SCHOOL FIELD TRIP ↱

SOCCER CHAMP ↱

TALKING TO SANTA ↱

FIRST INVISIBLE MAN ON THE MOON ↱

One picture is too big to fit in the album.
It's so big, it's hiding:

☐ Balloons (2)
☐ Bats (2)
☐ Birdhouse
☐ Birds (2)
☐ Boat
☐ Clock
☐ Coffeepot
☐ Covered wagon
☐ Crown
☐ Cup
☐ Dog
☐ Elephant

☐ Feather
☐ Fish (3)
☐ Fork
☐ Hearts (2)
☐ Horseshoe
☐ Jack-o'-lantern
☐ Jump rope
☐ Key
☐ Kite
☐ Mailbox
☐ Mermaid

☐ Old radio
☐ Old sock
☐ Old tire
☐ Pizza
☐ Tepee
☐ Worm

A MONSTER FAMILY PICNIC.

The monsters were so happy to have shared their ANCIENT FAMILY ALBUM with the kids, they asked the children to pose with them for a group photograph. However, before the picture can be taken, you must find:

- ☐ Bird's nest
- ☐ Bow tie
- ☐ Boxing glove
- ☐ Butterfly
- ☐ Camel
- ☐ Cow
- ☐ Crayon
- ☐ Deflated balloon
- ☐ Dinosaur
- ☐ Eight ball
- ☐ Elephant

- ☐ False teeth
- ☐ Fish
- ☐ Flying bat
- ☐ Football
- ☐ Football helmet
- ☐ Hamburger
- ☐ Hammer
- ☐ Igloo
- ☐ Kite
- ☐ Locomotive
- ☐ Model plane
- ☐ Mouse

- ☐ Music note
- ☐ Paintbrush
- ☐ Sled
- ☐ Slice of pizza
- ☐ Snake
- ☐ Tent
- ☐ Thermometer
- ☐ Top hat
- ☐ Wind-up car

Early one morning, Frankie has a brilliant idea. He thinks it would be great fun to visit some old friends he hasn't seen in a long time.

FIND FRANKIE IN HIS NUTTY NEIGHBORHOOD AND…

- ☐ Book
- ☐ Bowling ball
- ☐ Bucket
- ☐ Candle
- ☐ Dog
- ☐ Duck
- ☐ Fish (3)
- ☐ Flying bats (3)
- ☐ Football helmet
- ☐ Hammer
- ☐ Heart
- ☐ Jack-o'-lantern
- ☐ Moose head
- ☐ Periscope
- ☐ Pick
- ☐ Pinocchio
- ☐ Rain slicker
- ☐ Roller skates
- ☐ Sailor hat
- ☐ Scarecrow
- ☐ Skier
- ☐ Skull
- ☐ Snow shovel
- ☐ Star
- ☐ Tepee
- ☐ Thermometer
- ☐ Tulip
- ☐ Turtle
- ☐ Watering can
- ☐ Wreath

Frankie first looks for his old, old friend Manny Mummy in a place with lots of sand.

FIND MANNY MUMMY IN THE DRY DESERT AND...

☐ Balloons (3)
☐ Banana peel
☐ Bathtub
☐ Birdhouse
☐ Brooms (2)
☐ Earring
☐ Fire hydrant
☐ Fish (2)
☐ Flower
☐ Gas pump
☐ Ring
☐ Sailor hat
☐ Sand castle
☐ Sand pail
☐ Sled
☐ Slingshot
☐ Snake
☐ Snowman
☐ Soccer ball
☐ Star
☐ Straw
☐ Suitcase
☐ Surfboard
☐ Turtle
☐ TV antenna
☐ Umbrella
☐ Watering can
☐ Watermelon slice

Frankie and Manny Mummy set off to find their friend Batty Bat. He lives in a strange little town.

FIND BATTY BAT IN TERRIFYING TRANSYLVANIA AND...

☐ Alligator
☐ Arrows (2)
☐ Baker
☐ Bomb
☐ Bones (6)
☐ Book
☐ Bride and groom
☐ Broken heart
☐ Broken mirror
☐ Candle
☐ Dog
☐ Fish
☐ Flower
☐ Football
☐ Fortune teller
☐ Hair dryer
☐ Kite
☐ Lion
☐ Mouse
☐ Nail
☐ Octopus
☐ Rabbit
☐ Scissors
☐ Skulls (4)
☐ Top hat
☐ Training wheels
☐ Umbrella
☐ Vulture
☐ Wind-up monster
☐ Worm

Now they are off to find another old pal. This one lives in the heart of a swamp!

FIND SWAMPY SAM IN THIS MUSHY MARSH AND...

☐ Apple
☐ Barber pole
☐ Cupcake
☐ Drum
☐ Fish (5)
☐ Football helmet
☐ Fork
☐ Frog
☐ Grand piano
☐ Hammer
☐ Key
☐ Lost boot
☐ Lost mitten
☐ Medal
☐ Moon face
☐ Necktie
☐ Palm tree
☐ Pencil
☐ Pizza slice
☐ Ring
☐ Snake
☐ Soccer ball
☐ Sock
☐ Speaker
☐ Spoon
☐ Tent
☐ Toothbrush
☐ Trumpet
☐ Umbrellas (2)

Warren Werewolf is Frankie's next friend to find. He plays baseball with the Dead End Dodgers.

FIND WARREN WEREWOLF AT THIS BUMBLING BALLPARK AND...

☐ Bicycle horn
☐ Bone
☐ Cactus
☐ Camera
☐ Candy cane
☐ Carrot
☐ Cookie
☐ Crown
☐ Duck
☐ Empty can
☐ Eyeglasses (2)
☐ Feather
☐ Fir tree
☐ Flamingo
☐ Footprint
☐ Frog
☐ Heart
☐ Horseshoe
☐ Humpty Dumpty
☐ Kite
☐ Lamp
☐ Mouse
☐ Pliers
☐ Sewing needle
☐ Six-fingered glove
☐ Skull
☐ Squirrel
☐ Tick-tack-toe
☐ Whistle
☐ Witch
☐ Worm

Frankie and his pals go to an old schoolhouse where their friend Lena Lightning is a student.

FIND LENA LIGHTNING AMONGST HER CREEPY CLASSMATES AND...

☐ Apple core
☐ Bandage
☐ Bell
☐ Bone tree
☐ Broken mirror
☐ Cactus
☐ Candles (3)
☐ Crystal ball
☐ Egg
☐ Firecracker
☐ Flashlight
☐ Flying bats (3)
☐ Fortune teller
☐ Heart
☐ Hot dog
☐ Ice skate
☐ Mask
☐ Mouse
☐ Necktie
☐ Owl
☐ Pencil
☐ Pick
☐ Puss-in-boot
☐ Saw
☐ Shark fin
☐ Skateboard
☐ Skunk
☐ Snakes (2)
☐ Star
☐ Vulture
☐ Worm

Next, Frankie and his friends set out to visit Greta Ghost, but none of her neighbors have seen her in a while.

FIND FRANKIE AND HIS OTHER FRIENDS AT GRETA'S HAUNTED HOUSE AND…

☐ Alligator
☐ Arrows (2)
☐ Axe
☐ Balloons (5)
☐ Banana peel
☐ Bowling ball
☐ Broom
☐ Cup
☐ Dart
☐ Drum
☐ Flying bats (3)
☐ Fork
☐ Hammer
☐ Hatched egg
☐ Heart
☐ Keys (2)
☐ Ring
☐ Screwdriver
☐ Ski
☐ Skull and crossbones
☐ Stool
☐ Sword
☐ Teapot
☐ Tepee
☐ Torn sock
☐ Turtle
☐ Umbrella
☐ Water bucket
☐ Windsock
☐ Wreath

Frankie can't find Greta Ghost at the haunted house, so he and the others check the new condos and find her haunting there.

FIND GRETA GHOST IN MODERN MONSTERVILLE AND...

- ☐ Arrow
- ☐ Balloons (4)
- ☐ Bones (2)
- ☐ Cactus
- ☐ Camel
- ☐ Candles (3)
- ☐ Fire hydrant
- ☐ Firecracker
- ☐ Fish (3)
- ☐ Flowers (3)
- ☐ Football helmet
- ☐ Four-armed monster
- ☐ Frog
- ☐ Hoe
- ☐ Horseshoe
- ☐ Ice-cream cone
- ☐ Igloo
- ☐ Kites (2)
- ☐ Lollipop
- ☐ Lost bathing trunks
- ☐ Lost boot
- ☐ Mice (3)
- ☐ Painted egg
- ☐ Periscope
- ☐ Pyramid
- ☐ Quarter moon
- ☐ Rabbit
- ☐ Roller skates
- ☐ Seahorse
- ☐ Seal
- ☐ Sunglasses (2)
- ☐ Surfboard

Together at last, they all go on a picnic…where else but in a cemetery!

FIND FRANKIE AND HIS FRIENDS IN THIS GHOULISH GRAVEYARD AND…

- ☐ Apron
- ☐ Baseball cap
- ☐ Broom
- ☐ Burned-out candle
- ☐ Chef's hat
- ☐ Clothespin
- ☐ Crayon
- ☐ Crown
- ☐ Fish (2)
- ☐ Flower
- ☐ Fork
- ☐ Guitar
- ☐ Heart
- ☐ Hockey stick
- ☐ House
- ☐ Light bulb
- ☐ Mice (2)
- ☐ Paintbrush
- ☐ Picture frame
- ☐ Pig
- ☐ Ring
- ☐ Shovel
- ☐ Sock
- ☐ Spoon
- ☐ Straw
- ☐ Submarine
- ☐ Truck
- ☐ TV antenna
- ☐ Worm
- ☐ Wristwatch

After the picnic, Frankie and his friends go to see…you guessed it… a monster movie.

FIND FRANKIE AND HIS FRIENDS AT THIS FRIGHTENING FLICK AND…

- ☐ Apple core
- ☐ Arrow
- ☐ Clothespin
- ☐ Clown
- ☐ Dog
- ☐ Drum
- ☐ Eight ball
- ☐ Eyeglasses
- ☐ Faucet
- ☐ Fish skeleton
- ☐ Flashlight
- ☐ Football player
- ☐ Fortune teller
- ☐ Heart
- ☐ Ice-cream pop
- ☐ Moon faces (2)
- ☐ Necktie
- ☐ Oilcan
- ☐ Paper airplane
- ☐ Periscope
- ☐ Piggy bank
- ☐ Rabbit
- ☐ Roller skates
- ☐ Sailboat
- ☐ Skunk
- ☐ Star
- ☐ Superhero
- ☐ Top hat
- ☐ Trash can
- ☐ Trumpet
- ☐ Worm

While walking back from the movie Frankie and his friends see a frightening sight!

FIND FRANKIE AND HIS FRIENDS WITH THESE TERRIFIC TRICK-OR-TREATERS AND...

- ☐ Balloon
- ☐ Big lips
- ☐ Broom
- ☐ Butterfly
- ☐ Candy cane
- ☐ Carrot
- ☐ Chef's hat
- ☐ Crown
- ☐ Drumstick
- ☐ Earmuffs
- ☐ Envelope
- ☐ Fish
- ☐ Fork
- ☐ Key
- ☐ Lost sneaker
- ☐ Moustache
- ☐ Paintbrush
- ☐ Paper bag
- ☐ Pencil
- ☐ Pizza
- ☐ Roller skates
- ☐ Sailor hat
- ☐ Shovel
- ☐ Sock
- ☐ Squirrel
- ☐ Star
- ☐ Top hat
- ☐ Tree ornament
- ☐ Umbrella
- ☐ Watering can
- ☐ Worm

It's time for Frankie and friends to say goodbye… for now that is. They've planned to get together real soon and you're invited to join in the fun!

FIND FRANKIE, MANNY MUMMY, BATTY BAT, SWAMPY SAM, WARREN WEREWOLF, LENA LIGHTNING, GRETA GHOST AND…

☐ Apple core
☐ Arrow
☐ Baseball
☐ Bone
☐ Crayon
☐ Flowerpot
☐ Frog
☐ Heart

☐ Ice-cream cone
☐ Kite
☐ Owl
☐ Turtle
☐ Watermelon slice
☐ Worm
…and lots of other things.

Welcome to Creepy Castle, the castle that was never built. One moonless, creepy night it just appeared! Enter at your own risk! But first, find the following things hidden in this picture.

- ☐ Airplane
- ☐ Anchor
- ☐ Automobile
- ☐ Axe
- ☐ Bottle
- ☐ Broom
- ☐ Chair
- ☐ Clown's face
- ☐ Coffeepot
- ☐ Cup

- ☐ Duck
- ☐ Fire hydrant
- ☐ Fish
- ☐ Football
- ☐ Fork
- ☐ Hammer
- ☐ Heart
- ☐ Hockey stick
- ☐ Ice-cream cone
- ☐ Key

- ☐ Kite
- ☐ Paintbrush
- ☐ Pencil
- ☐ Ring
- ☐ Sailboat
- ☐ Screwdriver
- ☐ Star
- ☐ Toothbrush

WELCOME?

Racing through a partly open curtain, our friends enter the room of a famous monster star who's hidden all kinds of things. Can you find them?

- ☐ Automobile
- ☐ Axe
- ☐ Basket
- ☐ Bat
- ☐ Bird
- ☐ Bone
- ☐ Candle
- ☐ Cups (2)
- ☐ Elephant
- ☐ Fish
- ☐ Flower
- ☐ Guitar
- ☐ Hammer
- ☐ Heart
- ☐ Igloo
- ☐ Kangaroo
- ☐ Mermaid
- ☐ Mitten
- ☐ Moon face
- ☐ Mouse
- ☐ Party hat
- ☐ Pencil
- ☐ Rabbit
- ☐ Sailboat
- ☐ Star
- ☐ Toothbrush
- ☐ Tugboat
- ☐ Whale

Now there's a weird sight — a headless knight! Could he be related to the headless horseman of Sleepy Hollow?

Before going on, find these hidden pictures.

- ☐ Baseball bat
- ☐ Book
- ☐ Bottle
- ☐ Chicken
- ☐ Cow's head
- ☐ Cupcake
- ☐ Duck
- ☐ Eagle's head
- ☐ Ear of corn
- ☐ Envelope
- ☐ Feather
- ☐ Fish
- ☐ Fishhook
- ☐ Frog
- ☐ Ghost
- ☐ Hot dog
- ☐ Key
- ☐ Paper clip
- ☐ Pea pod
- ☐ Saw
- ☐ Shoe
- ☐ Slice of bread
- ☐ Sock
- ☐ Toothbrush
- ☐ Turtle
- ☐ Umbrella
- ☐ Wheelbarrow

What lurks beneath this new knight's hood? Is he a handsome hero or another creepy creature? Before you turn the page to find out, look for the following hidden pictures.

- ☐ Arrow
- ☐ Astronaut
- ☐ Banana
- ☐ Brush
- ☐ Cactus
- ☐ Carrot
- ☐ Crab
- ☐ Electric guitar
- ☐ Fish

- ☐ Heart
- ☐ Helicopter
- ☐ Hot dog
- ☐ Ice-cream cone
- ☐ Invisible knight
- ☐ Key
- ☐ Kite
- ☐ Magnet
- ☐ Parachute

- ☐ Pelican
- ☐ Rocket ship
- ☐ Sailboat
- ☐ Skis
- ☐ Star
- ☐ Teapot
- ☐ Toothbrush
- ☐ Truck
- ☐ Turtle

The newly knighted knight removes his hood and ... UGH! Put it back on! He sure is creepy!
Try not to look at him while finding the hidden objects in this picture.

☐ Automobile   ☐ Frog
☐ Banana   ☐ Hammer
☐ Bat   ☐ Key
☐ Beaver   ☐ Panda
☐ Bird   ☐ Pear
☐ Blimp   ☐ Pelican
☐ Book   ☐ Pencil
☐ Butterfly   ☐ Pyramid
☐ Camel   ☐ Ring
☐ Chair   ☐ Skunk
☐ Clown's face ☐ Snake
☐ Cow's head   ☐ Tent
☐ Cup   ☐ Tree
☐ Elephant   ☐ Turkey
☐ Fish   ☐ Turtle
                ☐ Umbrella

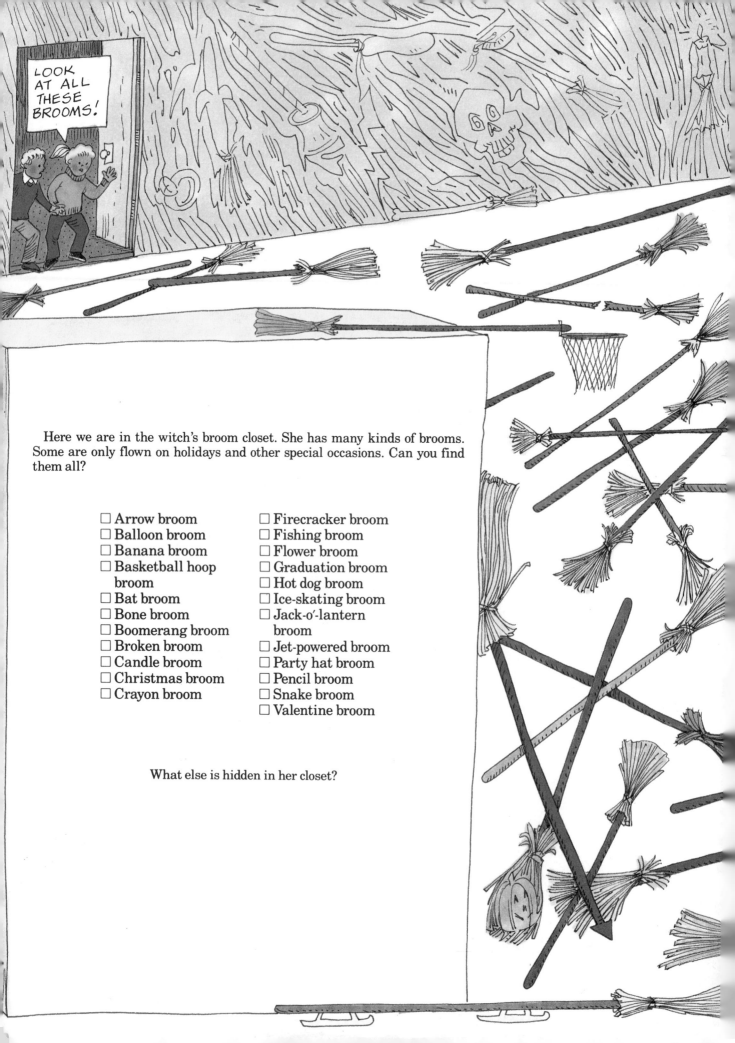

LOOK AT ALL THESE BROOMS!

Here we are in the witch's broom closet. She has many kinds of brooms. Some are only flown on holidays and other special occasions. Can you find them all?

- ☐ Arrow broom
- ☐ Balloon broom
- ☐ Banana broom
- ☐ Basketball hoop broom
- ☐ Bat broom
- ☐ Bone broom
- ☐ Boomerang broom
- ☐ Broken broom
- ☐ Candle broom
- ☐ Christmas broom
- ☐ Crayon broom
- ☐ Firecracker broom
- ☐ Fishing broom
- ☐ Flower broom
- ☐ Graduation broom
- ☐ Hot dog broom
- ☐ Ice-skating broom
- ☐ Jack-o'-lantern broom
- ☐ Jet-powered broom
- ☐ Party hat broom
- ☐ Pencil broom
- ☐ Snake broom
- ☐ Valentine broom

What else is hidden in her closet?

Through a hole in the wall, our friends take a peek at Wizard Merlin the magician, as he creates nasty nightmares.

Peek carefully at this picture and find the following hidden objects.

- ☐ Airplane
- ☐ Apple
- ☐ Arrow
- ☐ Axe
- ☐ Bat
- ☐ Drum
- ☐ Elephant's head
- ☐ Football
- ☐ Ghost
- ☐ Gorilla
- ☐ Hearts (3)
- ☐ Helicopter
- ☐ Horse's head
- ☐ Ice-cream cone
- ☐ Kite
- ☐ Lion's face
- ☐ Lizard
- ☐ Magnet
- ☐ Mask
- ☐ Mouse
- ☐ Mushroom
- ☐ Octopus
- ☐ Owl
- ☐ Paintbrush
- ☐ Shark
- ☐ Skull
- ☐ Snake
- ☐ Top hat
- ☐ Toucan
- ☐ Windmill

Surprise! Our fearless friends have been invited to a party in their honor. Looks like they're having a creepy, crazy good time!

You too can join in on the fun by finding the following hidden pictures.

- ☐ Arrows (2)
- ☐ Bat
- ☐ Bottle
- ☐ Cup
- ☐ Fish
- ☐ Flower
- ☐ Fork
- ☐ Ghosts (2)
- ☐ Hot dog
- ☐ Ice skate
- ☐ Key
- ☐ Kite
- ☐ Light bulb
- ☐ Mitten
- ☐ Music note
- ☐ Paintbrush
- ☐ Pencil
- ☐ Penguin
- ☐ Piggy bank
- ☐ Pinwheel
- ☐ Rocket
- ☐ Rocking chair
- ☐ Roller skate
- ☐ Seal
- ☐ Snake
- ☐ Sock
- ☐ Spoon
- ☐ Star
- ☐ Toothbrush
- ☐ Truck
- ☐ Umbrella

I WAS CROWNED PRINCE!

Congratulations! You have survived Creepy Castle! But what crazy gifts have our friends brought home?
See if you can find these peculiar presents. They are hidden in the picture below.

☐ Barbell
☐ Broken clock
☐ Cactus
☐ Cat
☐ Dog
☐ Fire hydrant
☐ Flying bat

☐ Fountain
☐ Heart
☐ Ice-cream cone
☐ Key
☐ Kite
☐ Lawn mower
☐ Pirate
☐ Pizza slice
☐ Ring

☐ Sailboat
☐ Sock
☐ Tennis racket
☐ Tent
☐ Tire
☐ TV set
☐ Umbrella
☐ Yo-yo